TikTok

Complete Guide to Growing your Followers, to Increase Fan, Became Famous and Generate Passive Income

---

MARK SIMON

TABLE OF CONTENTS

INTRODUCTION 1

THE CENTRIC INTERFACE DEFINITION. 4

UCD BACKGROUND TO MAXIMIZE CONSUMER. 6

THEORY FOR EXPERIENCE. 8

USER STUDY OF EXPERIENCE SENSORY. 10

ANALYSIS OF EMOTIONAL EXPERIENCE FOR USERS. 13

UGC AND PGC AND OGC CONTENT DEVELOPMENT BY
CONSUMERS TO SATISFY THE VARIED AND INDIVIDUAL
REQUIREMENT. 14

INNOVATIVE TYPES OF ADVERTISING TO APPEAL TO
CONSUMER NEEDS. 17

RECOMMENDED DEVELOPMENT ALGORITHM IMPROVES
PERSONALISED SUPPORT. 19

A COMMENT ON TIKTOK'S USER- CENTRIC CONCEPT. 21

TIKTOK A BEGINNER'S GUIDE. 23

    PHASE ONE: TURN THE PHONE'S VOLUME ON........................ 23

TIPS TO START ON TIKTOK... 29

FIVE DIFFERENT WAYS TO ROCK TIKTOK:................................ 31

    1. ITS SPECIAL NATURE AND SOCIETY-WELCOME IT. 31

    2. THIS ISN'T ABOUT PERFECTION—JUMP IN. 32

    3. TAKE THE CHANCE AND TRY-BE COURAGEOUS. 33

    4. RENDER DISCOVERABLE YOUR STUFF-HASHTAG IT. 34

5. IT'S WITH THE GROUP-APPROACHING THEM. 35

TIKTOK DEVICE MAKE SENSE. 37

MAKE A TIKTOK VIDEO. 38

HOW ALGORITHM WORKS WITH TIKTOK. 42

HOW TIKTOK'S ALGORITHM FUNCTION TO A CREATOR
CONTENT?. 43

HOW DOES TIKTOK COME TO KNOW YOU AS A USER?......... 44

TIPS ON MAKING VIDEO GO VIRAL. 46

HOW TO GET TIKTOK POPULAR PLAYING AND GAIN FURTHER
SHARES AND VIEWS. 48

PHASE 1: APPROACHABLE & CHARMING WILL SHOW TO
YOUR PROFILE. 49

PHASE 2: BE ON THE TIKTOK SUPER ACTIVE. 51

PHASE 3: ENGAGE IN CONTESTS & TOURNAMENTS ON
VIRAL TIKTOK. 54

HOW TO EARN MONEY ON TIKTOK. 56

INSTAGRAM. 63

SOCIAL MEDIA. 77

THE WORLD FOR SUCCESS MARKETING ON YOUTUBE,
FACEBOOK, TWITTER, AND INSTAGRAM. 77

THE SOCIAL MEDIA PROGRAM MARKETING, WHY DO YOU
NEED ONE. 83

PHASE 1: HAVE AN IMPRESSION ON YOUR SOCIAL
NETWORKING TARGETS. 83

PHASE 2: SOCIAL MEDIA PROFILES CREAT (OR SPRUCE UP OLD ONES). 86

PHASE 3: A LOT OF SPEECH BUILDING. 88

PHASE 4: TECHNIQUE GENERATING A MESSAGE. 89

PHASE 5: EXPERIMENT AND EVALUATE. 91

PHASE 6: PROCESS AUTOMATE, ENGAGE WITH FOLLOWERS, OR LISTEN. 92

TIPS ON FACEBOOK FOR MARKETING. 94

PROMOTIONS AND CONTESTS: MANAGING FACEBOOK. 103

TWITTER FOR BUSINESS. 105

TWITTER PLAN MARKETING. 109

YOUTUBE USING. 116

HOW TO CREATE A VIDEO. 121

CONCLUSION 125

INTRODUCTION

———————— ◆◇◆ ————————

A certain social networking service, called Musical.ly, has been extremely popular over the last few years. The key feature of the Musical.ly software was that users could build videos in tandem with background music or certain samples of audio. Some users used the device to make videos where lip locking and dance were involved.

The app was not only popular across diverse age groups of more than 100 million subscribers, but it also introduced new social media influencers to the fore. Musical.ly was formally shut down in November 2017 only as it was acquired by a Chinese firm named Bytedance. All Musical.ly users were moved to the new TikTok device, automatically. In 2016 a Chinese startup called Bytedance released TikTok. Bytedance made last year's sales of $2.5 billion, just like other companies in its place, it is also unprofitable. At over 40 million installs during three months in 2018, TikTok became the world's most-downloaded device.

As with Instagram and YouTube, people are also able to gain popularity and become influencers on TikTok. Users that achieve hundreds of views/likes are referred to as 'muser.' One downside often addressed by all is that TikTok offers no age limitations. It has been confirmed, however, that you will find several videos containing acts that mean self-harm or sexually explicit themes. As well as adults who use the software to harass and reach out to youngsters. Yet what are TikTok's key benefits? I checked the software a few days ago and will inform you of my feelings regarding the device now.

TikTok is reported to be a fusion of the two previous famous applications Musical.ly and Vine. The first thing I noticed was that you'll be showing different video clips as soon as you start the program that you may be interested in. Such an infinite video stream tab called 'For You' can instantly show clips identical to those you previously enjoyed. Throughout my situation, several of the seen videos were marked with Austria's hashtag. For first, however, I was not too entertained by the unexpected presence of those noisy videos.

Only using the magnifying glass icon once you're signed in and pick between common apps, background music, and hashtags. You'll just be given a hand-picked range of material under the 'Following' button. If you'd like to make your own 15-second movie, simply press the plus button. To add different filters or even slow down or speed stuff up, use the impact menu at the bottom of the left-hand menu bar. To create a lip-syncing picture, simply click on the musical note above. Click the 'Next' button and make some more changes, including incorporating hashtags, when you're pleased with your shot. You then click the 'Submit' icon.

I think that TikTok can be a lot of fun for teens in those days, but it doesn't guarantee it adults can love using this device too. I'm only 22 years old and I still got the impression I'm too mature for that stuff when using this device. This is just my perspective, some people may think differently. Nonetheless, this device will not be open to children under the age of 16. Everybody else will be very cautious of the videos they publish and you will never predict who is going to be able to view the footage. Although I definitely will not be utilizing this device, enterprises or organizations might also profit from this device in the future. Organizations will collaborate with a so-called 'muser' like for other influencers like Twitter or YouTube. Because of September 2016, TikTok has been available. In 2018, the number of average active users in China has already gone past 150 million, with more than 300 million active users each month. TikTok's overseas version has since been the most commonly updated in the world's Apple app store, with more than 500 million active users worldwide per month.

This can be assumed that citizens joined the TikTok age from around China. TikTok is the pioneer in the sharing network for quick music content, which focuses on vertical listen. TikTok is focused on the user-centric philosophy viewpoint, can improve user functionality, satisfy customer expectations, accomplish customer objectives, and draw users in-app layout design, content creation, and creativity generating areas, suggested algorithm technology centered on big data. To hold the customer, TikTok will help its users build interest.

THE CENTRIC INTERFACE DEFINITION.

— ◆ ◇ ◆ —

I n the digital media era, media-viewer interactions have moved from the core of the communicator to the middle of the consumer, and the viewer has moved from passive tolerance to aggressive content creation and sharing. Several researchers then brought forward the term "consumer" to substitute the term "audience." "User" is the active Data Client, Contact Member, Customer, and Product Entity, which is individualized rather than written.

"Central consumer" philosophy is to create the customer interaction as the heart, to take the user need as the reference, to take the user experience as the foundation, to find the user experience as the starting point and the inspection line of content production as an essential part of the development and output of media goods. "User-centric" philosophy is that TikTok improves the user's deep experience, reconstructs user relations, incorporates various situations to satisfy the user's communication exchange and speech needs, delivers personalized programs, aggregates capital, and generates interest.

That needs to retain the consumer and concentrate on the content's market value. TikTok APP's architecture is focused upon the user interface. The system architecture and digital architecture are aligned with the product users' location and preference. The content creation model is paired with the UGC and PGC and OGC style, which can produce mass content to fulfill users' varied needs, while the focused and vertical content meets users' specific needs. Macro story approach creative brief video material delivery and optimizes user interface. Its content creation and delivery of platforms are focused on Big Data Mining technologies and suggested an artificial intelligence algorithm that moves detailed details and offers personalized services to consumers.

Thus maximizing the customer interface, the development of knowledge cocoons. TikTok often pays undue attention to the consumer experience and the production of economic interest, it often contributes to a lack of direction on social meaning. The material includes vulgarization and homogenization drawbacks, and so forth. As a social communication platform.it, how to handle TikTok's social responsibility is worth reflecting on.

UCD BACKGROUND TO MAXIMIZE CONSUMER.

— ♦ ◇ ♦ —

User-centered design (UCD) aims at concentrating on the customer interface, desires, and goals. It also allows users to achieve targets, and to build interest. Customer interaction design involves user interface design (UI) and interactive design (ID) that provides trendy, innovation, and funky apps for young people. From the viewpoint of neuroscience and psychology, the consumer interface is optimized.

The interface design allows the human-computer interface method more compatible with the social needs of the citizens and defined priorities by formal design. The efficient form of engagement is used to accomplish the goal of maximum quality and improved user interface.

In 2006, Verplank, the founder in human-computer interaction, suggested that the secret to human-computer interaction would be the answer to "user-centric" human-computer interaction being the user interface, stressing the central role of the person in contact and the simplicity of understanding the program.

This shows in three aspects: thinking, understanding, and performing. The goals may be evaluated from accessibility and customer interface viewpoints, with an emphasis on people-oriented consumer needs. TikTok's digital user architecture is structured to demonstrate the features and benefits of the app. This will make it easy for consumers to use them in various situations, and provide potential users with a great initial experience. This helps them to come to grips with the commodity as quickly as possible. The architecture allows it possible for consumers to work easily by pursuing intuitions. At the same time, it also offers certain smart functionality such as live streaming to lure seasoned consumers.

THEORY FOR EXPERIENCE.

——————— ◆ ◇ ◆ ———————

B ack in the mid-1990s, customer interface designer Donald Norman introduced the idea of user experience (UE / UX). It's known as the user's whole feeling before, during, and after using a product or program. Those involve feelings, values, desires, attitudes, physical and psychological reactions, habits and successes, and other elements. As the consumer encounters TikTok, the term "consumer-centric" is expressed in the three dimensions of visual, contact, and emotion. TikTok's entertainment, excitement, and novelty all are emotional feedback.

The customer experiences a sensory impression that is fun and relaxed across a range of channel senses, such as listening and vision. The product type is an ethical experience that reflects the user's taste, status, and wealth. TikTok's motto is 'Records good life' As regards web delivery style, the vertical panel interface is more in line with the user's mobile phone reading habits, providing the "presence" immersive engagement.

As regards content development, the content production model of TikTok is coupled with the UGC and PGC and OGC system and also sets hot and challenging topics to improve user content output and viscosity. The brief video produced by the average citizen via the website accounted for nearly 49.1 percent, according to figures. 16 percent trend is consumers engaging in the platform's subject of challenges. Regarding the service of content, TikTok introduced the "see Music Program" to include effective and high-quality promotional platforms for young future original musicians.

The program not only enriches the wealth of their own music libraries but also optimizes the user interface. In the video clip part, it's doing their hardest to compensate for the uniqueness of the lifestyle of young people.

The video clip system is quick and fast to use, addressing the issue of advanced applications becoming challenging to use. There are all kinds of special effects like "clock gone" Different special effects were added, as well as fun filter effects. It is focused on the features of female users marginally higher than male users, and the enjoyment of fashion, appearance, and vitality by young people. Several special effects of "magnifying skin,-, whitening" render the video creation cycle more enjoyable, raise the Face Rating, and improve young women's attractiveness.

USER STUDY OF EXPERIENCE SENSORY.

———————— ◆ ◇ ◆ ————————

The processing of knowledge regarding the outer environment occurs from the visual organs, while the auditory perception applies primarily to the mental organ's perception such as sight and sound. The TikTok app's development design, feature implementation, and interaction design maximize the visual and auditory experience for the user. Development of the TikTok device layout, practical display, immersive architecture is designed to enhance visual and auditory interaction of the user.

(1) Visual and auditory architecture. The human brain is an efficient pattern processing machine that utilizes visual signals to control the amount of knowledge streaming through the mind. The graphic designer logically develops each aspect of the digital framework according to this trait, which more efficiently communicates the application's actions to the user. There's little interest from the men. The less time the consumer has to have to enter the digital code, the easier. The code will attempt to do away with useless details. Color and shape, animation of the details (video) may influence interaction. TikTok interface's black theme color and phonograph concept feature, in keeping with the trend and visual preferences of young people. Playing to see now just the home page of the consumer which simplifies the operating procedures. The post, like, tweet, share, rotate music CD and other icons get swift focus. It is flexible in architecture according to the

visual framework and satisfies the specifications of visual aesthetics. Additionally, several visual picture special effects combined with exciting and innovative music easily activate the user's auditory nerve.

(2) User Interaction Experience Analysis. Usability is the foundation of interactive design and provides a general assessment of availability. The interface's knowledge architecture and feature design meet the user's psychological needs and facilitate successful human-computer interaction. The design of the software system satisfies the psychological needs of the customer. The TikTok player GUI has a double tab above and below, a message bar on the right, shows text subjects, author comments, the music's initial sound in the bottom left segment, and so on. You will find the material on the site, if you are viewing, posting, socializing, adding, making your own stuff. User processes are more straightforward and smoother. Game cooperative device mode is easy and fast. For example, pull down to turn to the next picture, press Continue or Pause replay, and display the home page of the user on the left. The concept of a swift process saves the users time.

The specification of functions satisfies the specifications of different scenarios. TikTok fulfills user functions to scan, access, socialize, and build content.

(1) Feature to scan. TikTok understands the user and service search feature by configuring preload search technologies, including hot terms, search background, and "sweep a sweep" method.

(2) Click right away. The home page is the Player Gui and Automatic Loop preferred by default framework. The vertical style of play is in line with the visual senses.

(3) Work private. The GUI on the right hand has a button, such as focus, preferences, feedback, posting, etc. It has outstanding social
features by easily concentrating on others, understanding engagement with commentaries, exchanging valuable knowledge. TikTok
helps the viewer to comment and communicate with other users
without pausing video replay, and to perform social features as
well.

(4) The development role of UGC material. Users will create their own
video works instantly by clicking on the Build icon below. It also
provides editing and background music feature. Users will complete the custom editing of the video with a quick process to satisfy
the artistic needs of the viewer and share the achievement. From
the use scene point of view, the user will use the fragmentation period to interpret the details during the leisure time, whether it's the
shower, the room, the waiting time, or the time of travel.

ANALYSIS OF EMOTIONAL
EXPERIENCE FOR USERS.

———————— ◆ ◇ ◆ ————————

E motional experience is an occurrence through which awareness is used to guide psychology. This seeks to catch the interest of the individual and to trigger (conscious or unconscious) emotional responses to enhance the nature of the probability of executing certain behaviors. Attachment of consumer sentiment optimizes the user interface. TikTok's current ratio of male and female users, with 48.03 percent male users and 51.97 percent female users, is the same according to data. Users are mostly young people in age distribution, with the highest proportion being under the age of 30.

They're clustered in towns of the first and second tier. TikTok's hallmark is the brief music video, which blends the music's powerful linguistic capacity with the presentation of short video's popular culture power, which is compatible with the popularity of young people.

According to the survey, students at the college expressed high satisfaction with TikTok content's originality, fun, practicality, real-time, and freshness. TikTok has been remembered by users for transmitting the excitement and having fun, with the motto of capturing a happy existence. Young people often get the impression like they can't avoid surfing. This implicit subjective awareness catches the interest of the individual and increases the capacity to see TikTok.

UGC AND PGC AND OGC CONTENT DEVELOPMENT BY CONSUMERS TO SATISFY THE VARIED AND INDIVIDUAL REQUIREMENT.

◆ ◇ ◆

TikTok's user has more than 200 million in the second quarter, according to statistics. It has a large number of consumers. The content of TikTok's short video involves all facets of fashion, baby, cute cat, music, dance, food, travel, technology, gaming, entertainment, fitness, and so on. Its user-driven content production is the mechanism for generating mass content. That's the UGC and PGC, and OGC fusion phase. The material will only gain viscosity for the app because it will fulfill consumer needs. Communication theory of uses and gratifications claims that citizens are being allowed to fulfill those needs through any type of media. TikTok's content development becomes similar to the expectations of users' lifestyles, perceptions, and feelings, satisfying the users' psychological needs.

Through Maslow's hierarchy philosophy, that, having friends and attention, accepting value, is a higher degree of demand after fulfilling physiological and protection needs. The UGC mode content developer is an ordinary consumer and has no technical history. They build and share material focused entirely on personal observations and desires. For content creators, TikTok has almost no barrier. Users develop customized, dynamic, new, entertaining, and imaginative 15-second music video content focused on their own tastes, coupled with a range of enjoyable and fascinating songs, and unique effects and filters incorporated. It not only mobilizes the passion of users for content creation but also enables the TikTok platform to access vast content at very low cost and expand the type of content and the continuous flow of information. TikTok users' sense of engagement and sense of success often strengthen their commitment to it. As ordinary users create and consume content based on the same desires, contact and engagement may be formed with other users. This offers people a forum for the sharing of subjects to satisfy their social needs. Establishing social connections helps improve the platform's consumer stickiness.

The system of sharing has a significant impact on establishing social ties. TikTok produces content based on the UGC model which reflects its user activity and loyalty emphasis. PGC model content creators are persons or professionals of specific sector knowledge. We have some power and success in other areas, including fans of Wu Yi and other actors, novelists, foodies, authors, artists, etc. Based on their experience they deliver technical, insightful, vertical, and high-quality material. High-quality material is more appealing to consumers and can bring about the diversion of traffic. OGC model content creators are professionals of a degree of experience and technical context.

They generate content focused on the personal identification context and build interest across the web. For content creators, the OGC system establishes a higher level. It needs not only the skills or credentials of a specific sector but also the producer's professional identification. To a point, premium suppliers are selected to help generate material that is of better quality. The site believes "information is essential" and creates high-quality material to account for the UGC model's shortcomings. This will also fulfill consumers' specific desires to hold them, can their loyalty. The data interface is insistent on TikTok. It classifies users from the common, technical, and skilled perspectives to produce a variety of content that meets user needs. The application addresses users' specific desires through many forms of classification. Public users express their uniqueness through TikTok and establish social media due to the information fusion process of UGC and PGC, and OGC. Professionals like celebrities will increase their impact, and professionals may draw traffic and generate demand for their company. At the same time, the three improve the platform's appeal and engagement, which not only exerts the size benefit but also creates greater customer stickiness. Today the number of active daily users in China has already exceeded by 200 million. Not only does TikTok continue to extend the type and the scope and importance of content production, but it also enhances users' demand for content.

INNOVATIVE TYPES OF ADVERTISING TO APPEAL TO CONSUMER NEEDS.

— ◆ ◇ ◆ —

T ikTok is focused on a brief 15-second music video to compensate for the user's scattered interest. The quality of the brief 15-second video allowed the "mini-story" concept to innovate. The material includes plot characteristics, strong meaning, reverse, unorthodox, and imaginative. It mostly meets the interest of the customer.

According to US scholar E. M. Rogers, "innovation diffusion theory," refers to a "definition, process, or object" that is deemed new by an embracing entity, independently or otherwise. This spreads over a period of time across various networks amongst participants of a certain social community. The short video's novel narrative style has enhanced the content's speech and is much enjoyed by the public.

TikTok's project has been attempting to closely direct users' actions in content development. In the 1970s, the policy-setting hypothesis was developed by American persuasion theorist McCombs and Donald Shaw: there is a closely related connection between the public's perception and interpretation of important social public affairs topics and media reporting practices. This is, the "simple issues" mentioned by the newspapers are often expressed as "big stuff" in the collective consciousness.

TikTok's problems and hot topics illustrate the leading position that agenda-setting theory plays. The problems and trends inspire the netizens to build material and connect. It's quick to get the attention of millions and milliards of people. It can direct consumers in manufacturing material and enforce booting features. Under the guidance of specific topics, whether watching or participating in it, the user is concerned with similar content, providing a focus for the user to trigger common interests or actions.

Thus there is contact between the users of TikTok. The users' shared interest and participation also promote the exchange of each other's feelings. Tik-Tok regularly incorporates online hotspots to establish common themes including finger dance and seaweed dance. It allows people to build audio and video, and upload it. Hot subjects will attract interest from hundreds of millions of people.

RECOMMENDED DEVELOPMENT ALGORITHM IMPROVES PERSONALISED SUPPORT.

———————— ◆◇◆ ————————

McGuire, an English academic, argues that the conduct of the group is primarily clarified by human desires and preferences. The principle of uses and gratifications implies that viewers are people with different "demands" whose media communication activity is focused on particular motives "use" the platform, to "satisfy" their unique needs. The viewer should consciously pick and consider the material of the same purpose or meaning. The application of big data technology allows the media to better analyze and grasp the audience's different "needs" and provide corresponding services following their "needs." And it should maximize the experience of the customer.

The TikTok big data technology's insightful research is enabled by the strong data mining tools of Toutiao. The program displays the use of the media based on consumer preferences, sharing, length, class, age, place, etc. So it can measure the user's wealth, customer tastes, future needs, and other structured data in a reasonably detailed manner. The main technologies at TikTok are text mining, computer data mining, custom recommendation engines, and more. It allows for extensive data collection and recovery processing, confidential knowledge tracking, consumer experience analysis, and study review.

The website then offers goods and services to each customer that truly meets their needs. TikTok has a robust algorithm for transmitting video content in web delivery that fits its needs and preferences. TikTok has a thorough manual study of material delivery, in addition to sophisticated algorithms. Hundreds of users collate with the system to evaluate material and to suggest it. Manual checks make up for the mistakes in the computer algorithms. The app should reliably define users' functions, behaviors, and desires. The knowledge and material the audience likes is then driven depending on the tastes of the audience.

A COMMENT ON TIKTOK'S USER-CENTRIC CONCEPT.

————— ◆◇◆ —————

The website inappropriately fits the tastes of the consumer, culminating in the material becoming superficial and vulgarized. To understand traffic realization and market interest, TikTok is getting steadily superficial and obscene in material. Some of the content breaches the company's mainstream values, lacking effective and correct guidance on value.

The material is practically homogenized. Part of the material requires violations. Homogeneous and pleasant content is hard to maintain the long-lasting freshness and excitement of the user and is prone to aesthetic fatigue.

The moving material that consumers will easily lead to knowledge cocoons, as focused on suggested algorithm technologies. Users are only absorbed in their current framework and interests of knowledge which leads to unilateral and narrow information.

The party knows more for its own needs but can exchange "a feather's chickens" and would bring more cocoons of knowledge to the community. The user-driven system focused on the "user-centric principle" illustrates well the idea of "needs and gratifications." When there is just "satisfaction," and no "guidance" occurs, instead the role may decrease.

TikTok will stick to the position of "gatekeeper" and delete negative energy material as an answer to the vulgarity, shallowness, and web entertainment.

TikTok has to deliberately "place" those aspects of popular interest in the user-led and "private-custom" pop culture, to attain the role of guiding social values.

It can create a short social video platform with rich content, stylish taste, and entertainment. To prevent cocoons of knowledge, TikTok can include several video sources while distributing sources correctly to users. This will expand the horizons of consumers, and enhance their awareness. The platform's content creation adheres to "value is king" and deepens the PGC user development mode. By providing quality content, it can improve the aesthetic taste and satisfy the high-level spiritual needs of users.

TIKTOK A BEGINNER'S GUIDE.

— ◆ ◇ ◆ —

PHASE ONE: TURN THE PHONE'S VOLUME ON.

IT'S BEEN MORE than three years since the Musical.ly lip-syncing device, now known as TikTok, first became popular among tweens and teenagers. Since then the social network has expanded well beyond Generation Z: according to reports from the analysis company Sensor Tower, TikTok has been downloaded over 1 billion times, including 96 million in the United States. It's still operated by Bytedance, a Chinese corporation now deemed one of the world's most successful companies. The device itself is about exchanging 15-second video images, which are set to music that is regularly released by musicians and record labels. TikTok is now enjoyed not only by 14-year-olds in lip-sync, but also by actors, celebrities, and, indeed, labels. Big corporations such as Coca-Cola, Nike, ABC, and Google have been conducting promotional ads on TikTok. And Khloe Kardashian was compensated on the website for sharing supported posts. But the app's not only home to ads: TikTok is still ground zero for some of the most common memes on the internet. When you sound like you don't get TikTok you should be forgiven. The software is fast-paced and messy, merging Twitter, Instagram, Vine, and Twitch features into a cohesive media network. From TikTok "Challenges" to Coins and Original Sounds, here's what you need to learn to get started.

STARTING: SET YOUR ACCOUNT UP.

The first item you are going to require is a pair of headphones. There's no way to appreciate the sound off on TikTok. You will start viewing videos right away after you launch the device. But you'll need to sign up for an account to upload some yourself. You may use an e-mail, phone number or a third-party website such as Facebook to build an account. You are automatically assigned a username by the app. When you use your phone number to sign up for TikTok, the software can create a default username such as user1234567. Use an email address provides a more customized ID (though this may provide consumers with a privacy issue). Tap the icon in the right bottom corner to change your username, that looks like the upper body of a human. Then touch Profile Remix. Here you can transform it into something more special and add a story, image, and video profile. TikTok profiles are available by nature, so everyone can see your profile and display the videos you upload. Tap the three dots in the top right corner of your profile to adjust those privacy settings.

BROWSING TikTok.

It is time to catch some TikToks now that your profile is good to go. The software splits down into two different streams. The default is For You, a collection of videos created algorithmically, analogous to the Explore page of Instagram. Swipe left and you'll see the next page, Next, which features uploads from people you've picked. TikTok is like a variety show that never ends; it's pure entertainment. Follow developers who make you chuckle, like @k.chh, sharing funny skits, or then go for adorable accounts like @cute puppies12, uploading the smallest dogs I've ever seen. You'll find a set of icons to the right of any TikTok picture. The first one would take you to the user's profile which posted it. And there is a heart on Instagram which acts much like hearts or loves. Next are notes, then an arrow to the right to exchange individual TikToks with other sites. To share it on iMessage, for example, press the arrow if you want to copy the connection to a specific TikTok. (A warning for left-handers: you may consider TikTok tough to use, at least at first since it is always right-oriented.) The very last icon is a spinning record with music notes coming from it. It reflects the part of the music that the customer performs in their TikTok. Click on it to see the name and artist of the album, as well as a list of other TikToks which also feature it. E.g., over 1.4 million videos seen on the song's page featured "False ID" by Riton and Kah-Lo — an especially famous track on TikTok. Such clips are certainly not the complete scope of TikToks "False ID" on the website, but a little later more on that. Don't you want to see any kind of TikTok in your feed? Strong press to unleash a Not Interested button on the screen.

VIDEOS FROM RECORDING AND BROADCASTING TikTok.

Ready to share a TikTok of your own? Click the plus symbol at the bottom of the screen first. The camera opens, revealing a red record button resembling Snapchat. You should add a song before you start filming and your lip-sync, move, or skit is in time with the soundtrack. You can skip ahead and start filming without a musical track if you want to film something in the moment, then incorporate the music later on. Like with Snapchat, Tik-Tok has several AR filters that can be seen in images that include stuff including change hair color or eyes. Click Effects to browse on the left-hand page. The Planet tab contains socially conscious choices, such as a delicious-looking slice of augmented-reality pizza. Visual effects are planned for use on dogs and cats, too. There is a Beauty icon on the right-hand side of the camera pad, which gently erases the dark circles around the eyes. Below are the screen Filters. In comparison to Instagram, whose filters already have famous names such as Mayfair and Valencia, TikTok's are merely counted. The last and most significant feature here is the timer which enables users to film videos without holding down the record button continuously. That's what makes the iconic videos for TikTok dancing possible. TikToks can be up to 15 seconds long, but for up to 60 seconds of total video, users can also link several clips together. You can also post longer videos shot outside of the device itself. Start playing with duets until you learn standard TikToks, which break the screen in half and let you sing the same song as another writer. Tap the Share button on the original video to make a duet, and then hit Duet.

HASHTAGS, LYRICS, AND OBSTACLES.

Music is at the heart of TikTok; the primary reason a video goes viral could be to choose a famous album. Here's how to choose one. First, press Add a sound to the recording panel at the top. A Spotify-esque Musicians and Albums sharing menu will emerge. Here, you can search the platform's most famous albums, and check out Apple Music songs. There are no full-length songs on TikTok; short clips dominate the website, that can not be edited. In other terms, you might be out of luck if you think of performing the floss to a specific component of your favorite album. But there is a way to get around this problem. Many TikTok users simply play a song from a separate unit — like a monitor or stereo — when recording. TikTok can then record the track as "original music," which can then be applied to their own videos by other users. A word of caution: Copyright infringement can result from using this workaround. The songs affiliated with TikTok #Challenges are on the same online music page. Challenges are what tie the TikTok culture together, and marketers also fund them. E.g., ABC is running the #LikeAnAmericanIdol challenge on TikTok right now, which invites you to "show off your stunning speech!" "(To date, 25.3 million hashtag videos have been created.) Google recently conducted a similar hashtag #HeyGoogleHelp challenge campaign. The majority of the challenges are not sponsored. They're produced instead by TikTok and the group itself. E.g., the #faketravel challenge currently features in the app, in which users claim to be on a lavish holiday. The image is poking fun at influencers on other sites including Instagram who brag about their #jetsetlifestyle. Tap the magnifying glass at the bottom of the home screen to browse through all of TikTok's current challenges. There's a search bar at the top of that very page, which can be used to check for unique writers, sounds, or hashtags.

VIDEOS, NOTES, AND OTHER INDICATORS.

If you start posting TikToks, by looking at the display numbers on your profile you can test how many people have been watching them. To see who has posted or enjoyed your posts, press the updates button at the bottom of the home screen. You will see who stared at your profile or followed you here too. One significant tip: TikTok is infamous in the context of push alerts for sending communication bait hoards. Should that kind of spam sound unattractive, toggle off TikTok alerts in the settings menu of your computer. TikTok often notifies users when "LIVE streaming" is famous creators (this function isn't open to every user). As on Twitch, you can tip makers through interactive items that are bought with TikTok Coins when viewing a live stream. $1 = one hundred coins. Creators also remember their customers or address questions they pose in return for certain items, a part of which may be translated into daily currency.

WHO IS A NORMAL USER OF TikTok?

Besides its intriguing history tale, TikTok has some important demographics as well. The bulk of the consumers are female according to estimates. But still, 66 percent of all consumers are less than 30 years old.
This makes TikTok an app that any parent should learn about right away. If
you think your kid is too small for the material of TikTok, you may want to
look into ways to make your smartphone more child-proof. At the moment,
TikTok draws more and more viewers beyond its planned profile of "lip-
syncing 13-year-olds." Social networking influencers, famous launches,
comics, and major brands have been having the spotlight too. Nike, Coca-
Cola, and even Google are among those businesses that have already begun
ads inside the device. More funded content emerges on the network and this
is a sign of progress. Since TikTok is the starting point of many famous
memes and challenges, it is also extremely common among millennials.

TIPS TO START ON TIKTOK.

———————— ◆ ◇ ◆ ————————

"Well finished, boomer! "Huh, huh? What one is a boomer? "I'm ooping ... sksksksk?!?! "How does this say even? What's a kid on VSCO? "Peppa, what is it that you do? "Wait, there are so many uncomfortable positions taken by an animated pig? Do you ever feel like listening to an album, and do you not understand the lyrics? You are not alone in this. For me, it has felt like 2019. During Google's Year of Search, jargon from a recent quick video-based social networking site has become some of the most sought-after words. Brands, actors, and advertisers have been flocking to TikTok during the past 6 months, catching the attention of more than one billion active users across the globe.

Why? For what?

A big explanation why advertisers, celebrities, and marketers follow Tik-Tok is that 60 percent of consumers are under the age of 30—consisting of both Gen-Z and Millennials who are the biggest demographic community with an expected buying power of $1.4 trillion by 2020. Another explanation why advertisers, celebrities, and marketers hop on the bandwagon is that the algorithm will make anybody's video go viral irrespective of how many followers the user might have. That implies that this is a fantastic place to be discovered and an opportunity to expand. Now that you've got an idea about why so many labels, celebrities, and advertisers flocked to TikTok.

There are three major forms in which labels, celebrities, and advertisers may use TikTok:

- Build their own TikTok profiles, and upload videos regularly.

- Partnering with authors to build and/or distribute original pieces of material with a larger audience. This can be achieved by going out and personally collaborating with developers, by utilizing the Artist Platform of TikTok.

- Leveraging TikTok's paid promotional goods for brand marketing, facilitating e-commerce sales, enabling engagement, etc. As the company is fairly young they actively develop and introduce innovative ad-related items for popular companies, actors, and advertisers.

Many companies, actors, and advertisers are actively integrating both strategies and experimenting to see what resonates most with their audience(s), which can propel their activities to the highest direct and indirect benefit.

FIVE DIFFERENT WAYS TO ROCK TIKTOK:

———————— ◆ ◇ ◆ ————————

1. ITS SPECIAL NATURE AND SOCIETY-WELCOME IT.

TikTok is a collective. It does have traditions and rules. The atmosphere varies from that of other sites. Which runs on Facebook, on TikTok, may not work. And then vice versa. Take your time poking around. Look beyond what creators do to see how they do it, and why they do it. Knowing and welcoming the culture will help you realize where you belong. You will see creators' weird, fun creations that will make you repeat their videos more than once, all the while wondering "What am I watching? "You're going to watch cringe-worthy images that will have you embarrassingly wonder why I just did it? "There's everything. There are so many opportunities to engage in the group, from lip-synching to juggling and competitions to duets, it'll be easy to find what works for you — that's why TikTok is addictive.

#PROTIP: If you haven't already created an account, download the app but don't set up an account. And instead, on various occasions, spend a couple of days opening the device and seeing what's going inside. Monitor videos in your "About You" list, discover the problems of the hashtag, and check about accounts you are involved in (to see who they are following). TikTok allows you to access the material without logging in. You're not going to be allowed to do stuff like heart or tweet, but the software does not completely configure depending on your preferences, ensuring you're going to enjoy a broader variety of content. And most significantly, you'll continue to know the dos and don'ts when you click through TikTok. Don't erase remarks. Or limit the sharing of your images. Don't only toggle on duets, but challenge your fans to deliberately duck your photos. If you borrow a concept from another artist or use the audio, don't forget the initial author, offer them credit. Then doing such stuff would make it look as though you're only on TikTok to transmit your material as a company, celebrity, or marketer. But by opening up your material to everyone to interact with, showing you recognize and respect the standards and traditions, and taking part in the numerous videos, patterns, and hashtag challenges, you'll prove not just your audience but the wider TikTok culture that you're right there with them. That you love the culture and recognize it.

2. THIS ISN'T ABOUT PERFECTION—JUMP IN.

The single greatest factor a lot of people don't continue producing videos is that they're searching for perfection. People believe they need to create high-quality images. They believe that to produce content they require perfect lighting or a professional-level camera — which is not accurate. What TikTok's success has shown is that it's the actual content of the video that counts most, not the manufacturing. Millions are already noticing the silly stuff that we do while we are in front of the bathroom mirrors or drive in our cars alone across town.

And while you may like to see your videos in any form (and it's great if you're taking the time and effort), it's not important — and frankly, it's better to just continue. Decide if you want to share and document anytime you can, or anywhere. Brands may achieve that by showing off a skill with a company personality or community of staff, performing a tune, ruling the dance floor, making a joke or two, conversation with lip-synch videos, or almost something. It's more necessary to contribute than to excellence.

3. TAKE THE CHANCE AND TRY-BE COURAGEOUS.

If you're spending enough time on TikTok you'll see some of the strangest and funniest stuff you've ever seen. You should completely engage in the group by joining in on videos, events, and hashtag competitions, as has been discussed above, but you should never feel limited. Don't fret. Chances carry. I do this by making the opportunity for us to understand I know.

Find your peer brands or famous developers and see what they do — follow their public indicators to see what works and what doesn't work. Spend your time not only staring at their latest material but reaching further and examining how their material has grown over time. See which videos stand out from the others; follow trends that can aid in your efforts. Look at the number of views a user is getting by doing so.

First look at how many hearts/likes, reviews, and posts there are. Then ask questions:

a) Do people watch the video? ; and

b) Will the video interact/engage their audience? If the response is "yes" to both instead worry about what those findings are doing.

Is it the Maker? Was that the point? Is it the locations, or the type of production? Getting peer feedback like this helps companies, actors, and advertisers to learn what succeeds for them and why it succeeds. You will consider videos or hashtag competitions that you will be able to incorporate into your content offerings. And you'll see something truly unique to that company or maker and that's not going to work for you. You're going to start getting a taste about what to show the crowd and what to play with.

4. RENDER DISCOVERABLE YOUR STUFF-HASHTAG IT.

When TikTok's exponential development continues as more and more labels, celebrities, and advertisers enter, it will become increasingly difficult to find your content. Hashtags on all social networks are important but hashtags on TikTok are crucial. They are pushing obstacles, videos, and also sharing tales. Perhaps most critically they improve discoverability — the opportunity to locate the material for others. TikTok requires the captions to have minimal character duration so keep the text brief and consider incorporating 4–6 hashtags. Two or three hashtags should be specifically linked to your video and the other hashtag types like #tiktoktravel should be more common.

Be alert, stop hashtag-jacking — the habit of utilizing irrelevant famous or trendy hashtags to attempt and get the posts published. This looks like a vain effort to be noticed and will turn the fans off. In addition, TikTok is searching for certain "sweet terms." Think about terms relating to human sexuality, sexual relations, words about cursing or hatred, or certain vocabulary that might be considered unacceptable for certain audiences. You will have the videos marked and deleted if you include certain words in the captions.

If one of your videos is deleted, take a glance at the description and see if it contains a term that may have been noticed (for starters, we've had a cooking video taken down in the description of a chicken dish being cooked for using the term "breast"). Here's a case study by The Drum with a deeper look at how a company used a paying hashtag contest, unique immersive augmented reality (AR) screen, and TikTok developers to support a campaign, instead of instances.

Case Study: A hashtag campaign entitled "Smile Campaign" was introduced by the Colgate-Palmolive company to demonstrate how happiness can be turned into motion and a smile represents one's happiness. The initiative spanned six days targeting India, Malaysia, Singapore, Thailand, and the Philippines. Colgate released a custom smile sticker that can sense the expression of the TikTok customer, and practically score it.

To seed the initiative, the company asked 100 TikTok content creators to film and submit videos to the challenge in the five nations, enabling their fans to submit their own versions of the challenge. The initiative named "Smile Challenge" created 1.6 M user-generated images, 2.5B of overall content views. For the songs, it said that there were 53,000 user-created videos and a total of 26 M video views.

5. IT'S WITH THE GROUP-APPROACHING THEM.

All that you do on TikTok is for the crowd. You are seeking to draw on the forum as well as strengthen your experiences with them. Lets them know you. Having them to communicate with you on TikTok and off. But don't just transmit or view them as inactive fans, set aside time to contact them. Relationships grow and cultivate. Decide on a plan of communication by putting aside the time to view videos from the community — and not all the pages you track. Determine what sort of stuff you're searching for, what you admire most, and how to better convince designers that they've drawn your interest or just inspired you to comment or share. Through joining their content, you can only help to bring more viewers to see their images, but you may also encourage them to respond with your heart's joy and excitement, tweet or subscribe.

#ProTip: don't just heart / like a post after seeing the entire thing, if you do so it could have a detrimental effect on the credibility of that user by having the credibility marked by the site as though it were an artificial or inauthentic interaction activity that might happen to any specific video or author. It may have an effect on the distribution of their videos or even on the overall account of the maker.

Seek to engage with as many constructive messages as possible on your own videos and maybe addressing a Direct Message (DM) or two on occasion. Interact with them and analyze the material with them, seek reviews, and function to build in those fields. TikTok rewards this action in several ways, as you communicate with the audience. Yeah, it may all be a little daunting. With its nuances and new jargon, TikTok will sound like a completely other planet. Yet it is much like any networking media before it. It is a group of deeply motivated designers who share themselves and interact with other people from all over the planet. You're going to catch on, very quick-pledge.

At the very least, whether you're a company, celebrity or marketer get on the forum and start listening to what's being said about you and defending your intellectual property by posting your name(s) for your page.

TIKTOK DEVICE MAKE SENSE.

———————— ◆ ◇ ◆ ————————

O kay, create no fear. The For You stream should be a relatively random hodgepodge of links before you start following a few users or like images. So start scrolling to see what you find, or you can continue by synchronizing your contacts to find your friends using the app in the Follow area.

The Explore tab is a fantastic place to find stuff, too. See what popular hashtags are to figure out what you're involved in. If you like a picture, press the heart button or double-tap it. Most of the places you will communicate with a video are on the right side of the screen — the profile of the user, the "like" button, the comment area, the sharing features, and the spinning icon that will display you any videos featuring that specific song. If you long-press the screen you can save a picture, add it to the list of your favorites, or claim you are not interested in it.

You may even swipe left to reach the creator's profile. You will track the designer from there. The style is identical to Instagram in that it's only images, and it's not meant to be too exotic. You will find likes and feedback from your fans on the Notifications page when you become more interested in the forum and connect with more users. The Updates tab even contains your private message inbox. Click the profile icon and then the three-dot options in the top-right corner to make some changes to your account, including privacy settings or email alerts for example.

MAKE A TIKTOK VIDEO.

———————————— ◆ ◇ ◆ ————————————

P repare for the first video? Click the white "+" in the middle at the bottom of the screen to grant TikTok the requisite approvals it needs. You may either post a picture or record something different. I put my cat's old Snapchat video into a dresser drawer so why not? After posting you will cut a video instantly. You should only feel fancy now. Your tools for sound recording are at the top right, and the settings for video editing are at the bottom left of the computer.

Click Choose Sound in the top right-hand corner to add a song to your message. From there, playlists, fame, or hashtags will scan for the tracks. Tap the red checkmark to add it, until you've reached the right song. Using the Mixer or Trim tool to get the album exactly the way you like it. By clicking the three-colored button at the bottom of the page, or by swiping left, you may use simple filters. To add the stickers, GIFs, or emojis, press the smiley face. Many of the adhesives are animated.

If you have lost one in your picture, you can move it into place or, if you want to erase it, to the top of the screen where tiny trash can appear. Click Effects to move the video to the next point. Here you'll find more visual filters including Rainbow, Air, Snow, and Feathers to drop over your video. The best thing is that as soon as the video helps you will adjust the filters. To add it simply long-press on a filter and let it pause. Tap Stickers to attach facial filters Snapchat-style to the video. Through Effects, you will add Spin, Rotate, Slide, and more transformations. Tapping Split, well, breaks the panel up to nine directions whenever you wish. Eventually, you can apply reverse effects to the video, flash (like a double- or triple-take), or slow motion. Tap Click Cover to create a snapshot so others can see when they discover your file before you post it. Are you ever dizzy? If your video is up for grabs, press Next. The Publishing screen is close when you use Instagram. There is a text box that helps you to write a bit about your picture, add any hashtags or tag mates.

Tap Who Can Access This Video to configure your tastes, and pick between public, friends only, or private (meaning you can just see it). You may even turn on or off comments. Save the video to previews, upload it to Twitter automatically or only submit it to TikTok. Whatever privacy settings you have chosen for this specific video, TikTok will seek confirmation before uploading. You can see a message letting you know that your account is public and that any shared upload is available to everyone. TikTok goes on to inform you about the settings for private account choices. In a separate warning, TikTok also states that even though all of your settings are private, your videos do need to meet the rules of the group. Go search your profile for a picture of your uploaded photo.

THAT'S GREAT, BUT HOW DO I GET FAMOUS?

Although internet fame may seem simpler than ever, there's nothing we can guarantee. It's pretty uncommon to see a one-off video going viral and sky-rocketing an individual into internet success, but here are some general tips that will bring you to a verification badge in no time.

1. Write plenty. Just pretty much. If you luck out of the gate on a viral video and keep the traction, it requires time and effort to create a profile on TikTok. Build your schedule so you are posting frequently enough to create a steady stream of material. Do not be scared of livestreams, either; seek to do them only once a week.

2. Figure out what you're good at. Sadly, a lot of people are fantastic at the same stuff and the internet is massive. Looking for the little aspect to set your videos apart from everyone else's when you continue on your quest towards internet fame. The larger the gap, the stronger. Hold things simple until you hit your stride. One day don't perform a beauty demonstration and instead, explain how to repair a television the following.

3. Create professional images. You don't have to go to the film school but you can deliver a professional product if you're serious about building an online presence. You wouldn't want to support someone who doesn't even upload decent photos, right? Don't go bankrupt on video gear, but instead invest in a digital tripod (they will cost as low as $5 at Staples or $8 at Amazon). Read up on the structure of videos when you are on the checkout track.

4. Using social media to communicate. Odds are, if any of your social networking sites are tied together you'll have more success. The more social networking sites you're in, you'll be much luckier. You are currently pro-moting your favorite celebrities and influencers on different sites, but wouldn't you want to do the same with your followers? Further channels to join implies further access to the images, and a wider market to target. That said, don't gamble on Internet celebrity for your health. Building a Finsta and creating your own private Instagram maybe. Additionally, you will build a Profile on Facebook if you have enough fans, and keep your page secret.

5. Follow for follow. It's a great deal to connect with your people. You know how fun it is when you retweet your favorite podcaster, or a celebrity, or you want that Instagram message. Any reason to offer the cold shoulder to somebody. When they're posting on one of your articles or a photo, like it and back click. Hold health in mind of course, as always. Many critical reviews can be positive and they will help you develop your content; because you are in the general spotlight, not everyone would enjoy what you're doing. Certain remarks or tweets may be threats, grumbling, and violent. Using flexibility. Document the bullies, and delete them. Do not hesitate to connect with other developers of TikTok too! How is it they are getting right?

6. Do the reading. What's popular on every social networking site is essential to the performance of a picture. In the Discover page, pay attention to hashtags, what's common right now and what's happening. It would seem to contradict the "find your stuff" idea, but you should put a hashtag on your video to make it more retrievable — so it doesn't need to be based on the hashtag. The more meaningful the content is, however, the more it would do for the audience.

HOW ALGORITHM WORKS WITH TIKTOK.

———————— ♦◇♦ ————————

T he social media world is dramatically shifting. The social money that compensated web developers and influencers has become an asset in follow-ups and shares over the last decade. TikTok's short-form video software has introduced a modern approach that utilizes an ever-changing algorithm to determine whether its customers are consuming. Tik-Tok is incredibly good at suggesting content, so much so that when a consumer opens the device, they would be remaining with it for more than 10 minutes on average. Four times as many as Facebook. It indicates that decisions focused on algorithms are much stronger than humans utilizing filters including and obey. When the technology and user-based philosophy of TikTok evolves, we should anticipate this recommendation system to get a lot better over time. It's been well established for a long time that vertical short-form smartphone video should be the future of web content. Snapchat achieved early popularity in this sector with images and video vanishing, and instead their revolutionary style of news. Nevertheless, with its mix of native short-form content and algorithmic suggestions, TikTok is at present winning over global viewers. In this article, we will seek to unpack to the best of our understanding how this technology operates, with both users and content developers alike. Through knowing the dynamics behind the network, we will continue to use that to help guide our decisions about content production and start drawing potential future improvements to the environment. To non-technical writers, please remember this is a high-level message. Please remember also that we should assume hundreds if not thousands of specific suggestion algorithms to operate at any point in time. Good to go!

HOW TIKTOK'S ALGORITHM FUNCTION TO A CREATOR CONTENT?.

This is how you judge a video when it's shared on TikTok. After downloading a file, TikTok analyses the file utilizing natural language processing techniques and computer vision. The details should be taken from the video itself to explain the material, audio, transcriptions to create an understanding of the background and meaning of the videos. Here's a line from Bytedance describing how the technology works: "Artificial intelligence drives all the web channels of Bytedance," says the spokesperson. "We develop intelligent machines that use natural language processing and computer vision technologies to interpret and evaluate text, pictures, and videos. This helps us to provide consumers with the material they consider most compelling and inspire creators to express experiences that appeal to a global audience in daily life. "Now that TikTok knows the facts about the app, it is going to improve the app to a limited number of users. After booting the video an assessment would take place depending on how the user's sample collection deals with the content object. Every parameter that is monitored has a value-varying associated ranking. Here is a hierarchy of approximate ranking, which rewards material per user experience.

* Relook levels = 10 Marks.

* Rate to total = 8 Marks.

* Stocks = 6 Dollars.

* Remarks: 4 rows.

* Likes = 2 Objects.

As you can see from the above, per-user interaction ratings are the top-rated indicators and are juxtaposed to the least likes and reviews. Leaving a video running on a loop, though, does not allow the videos to go viral, because it is measured per device. This rating structure renders click farms obsolete, Facebook has dealt with an issue for some time. You can now link the video to a ranking. When the content is over a level than more TikTok users would be enhanced. Again and again, the cycle continues until it goes viral, or before it no longer reaches the level of TikTok. Not all posts will, therefore, be crafted for viral purposes. Attracting the correct consumers is far more valuable for the app than targeting millions of people who don't relate to the site.

HOW DOES TIKTOK COME TO KNOW YOU AS A USER?

TikTok wants to read about you as much as possible so that she understands what material to support you. When a user first installs TikTok, they open the device and drop straight into the video feed without signing up. As well as being a perfect Ui choice, it reduces the entrance threshold but is a wise one from a data collection point of view. From this stage, the software starts thinking about you as best as it can. The first series of videos you're watching now is supposed to do two things.

1-Hold yourself in the game. The first job is to hold you as long as possible inside the device. Showing you only videos that are rated as providing strong levels of interaction to a large audience, while still getting the lowest rate of exit.

2-Comprehend what you seek. The second is to know what you are getting from the pool of images. Which videos do you replay on a loop again, what is your rate of completion per picture, what accounts, hashtags, and patterns do you look at? TikTok's algorithm should now start creating a score-based profile against your account utilizing the same method as previously. Every time you rewatch a video or ingest the video's entire length, the algorithm takes care of reminding its potential recommendations. Again, here's the point scheme.

* Review = 10 Marks.

* Rate of completion = 8 rows.

**Actions = 6 Points.

* Remarks = 4 Marks.

* Likes = 2 objects.

Through time this profile is more and more educated, so that material can be best tailored to your needs. Place, period, and day would also fall into the suggestion algorithm, much like conventional TV programming. In this article, however, we do not discuss these facets of the algorithm.

TIPS ON MAKING VIDEO GO VIRAL.

───────── ◆ ◇ ◆ ─────────

The previous parts clarified the Matching Engine algorithm for Tik-Tok, and when uploaded, the flow of a video goes through. Let's now go through those ideas to help get the videos more popular.

1. RATIO TO COMPLETION. The Completion Ratio, as described earlier, is the percentage of the video viewers viewed, which is the most significant output rating metric as the algorithm decides how to send it to more viewers. Below are few suggestions to better inspire people to view a whole movie, and maybe repeatedly:

1.1. 10 to 15 seconds video length: shorter videos raise the likelihood for viewers to continue and not interrupt owing to a lack of attention span.

1.2. Seamless loop video: Seamless loop videos improve viewers' likelihood of viewing it several times, as it benefits the completion ratio because it is viewed as continuously watching a video.

1.3. Teaser video: Teaser video provides suspense so fans want to know what's happening at the edge. This method is used in videos that use words like "Watch for it" or "See what happens next."

2. MUSIC TO THE THEME. Creators will increase their chances of seeing a video sent to more audiences easily by using songs that many fans have previously liked.

3. HASHTAGS RISING. Within the video summary, producers should use common hashtags in the same manner as utilizing popular songs.

4. QUESTIONS POSE. In the video raise a query where users are invited to participate with feedback. Make sure you like those comments and respond to them to create a conversation and raise commitments.

5. BUILD A CULTURE. We encourage followers to add to potential video material and feel like they're part of the community.

6. JUST ADD 1–2 VIDEOS A DAY. Restrict uploading to one or two videos a day — no more, and the system would look at it as spam, and stop pushing the images. Furthermore, fans of the same channel are less likely to interact with more than a few videos every day.

7. BEST HOURS FOR WRITING. The optimal posting hours are early evening (6 pm) and midday (12 pm), in that order, where consumers of the periods will be surfing on the web. It may be different based on regions and countries, but our history has shown that these are the best periods for the USA.

HOW TO GET TIKTOK POPULAR PLAYING AND GAIN FURTHER SHARES AND VIEWS.

◆◇◆

TikTok is one of 2019's most downloaded games, which has 1 trillion Google Play store updates. Wanna be featured on TikTok? Or on your TikTok page, you want to get more followers? Yeah, so you find the right post, all of this stuff I'm going to cover in this section. With these tips, I'll explore how you can be popular on TikTok. Honestly, I just enjoy TikTok, I'm one of the top TikTok Users' biggest fans and that's what makes my legs go jelly for being popular and those hearts you get when a girl likes you or supports you. Yeah, I really can't understand that. Somebody tells me, are these people the professional actors? I inform them, to render these material looking almost flawless takes a lot of hard work.

How to Get More Views and Likes on Your Videos: Use the following five-point strategy if you want to get more likes and support on your TikTok posts. This is the full method I use for my TikTok posts. Here's how you should use this five-point to assemble your videos more:

1. Add Links to your videos: To get more impressions and visibility, apply Trending marks.

2. Look fine. Look beautiful. Whoever you are, look good and you're going to receive more attention, it means more views on your TikTok videos.

3. Take patience before making videos: creating the right clip requires a lot of effort, taking several photos before picking the correct one.

4. Post the Quick TikTok videos on Other Channels of Social Media.
Since TikTok has more than 1 billion users, there's a high probability the
individual would land on your website.

5. Find a niche, and keep to it. You can't do anything and it's easier to stick
to a subject and create videos relevant to that subject.

I interviewed a guy who has more than 1 million followers and according
to him and a few other people I've encountered to find out what's the secret
to having other hearts (Likes) and Views and followers on the TikTok app?
I like this device, and want to see what impact it can have on the community
and bring improvement. I've recruited some of the tips and strategies on this
quick video creation device to gain more shares and followers.

PHASE 1: APPROACHABLE & CHARMING
WILL SHOW TO YOUR PROFILE.

If you want to go viral on TikTok, one of the items that's important to make
sure your profile is appealing. Each bit of knowledge is important and helpful when it comes to optimizing your profile. Your username, profile picture, and personal details will all leave a positive impact on someone who
visits your page. E.g., a lengthy, hard to remember username won't help you
win further popularity. That's because most definitely a lot of people would
overlook it right after they hear it.

Through utilizing a fun, exclusive, yet fast username, one way to excel here
is If you're still an influencer on other sites like Instagram or Twitter, seek
to create the same TikTok username. This way, migration to TikTok is simple for your current followers. It's important to use this space when it comes

to your TikTok Bio Space to show yourself, your material, or your objectives. For example, if you're creating niche comedy material. Introduce yourself and the knowledge you have in the industry, through live shows maybe people will recognize you. If this is not up to your liking, compose a brief note about the comedy style you usually make.

Finally, you may use the bio-space to position CTA's to motivate the crowd to conduct a particular action. Your profile is the very first move in establishing contact with followers. You must take advantage of the opportunity to connect with followers. That is why you need to put a lot of effort into persuading new followers to join you and start interacting with you.

1. LOOK BEAUTIFUL IN YOUR VIDEOS: that's what makes us different. That is what calls for personalities. The cooler and more appealing you feel the more people expect to view and post your videos with their peers. According to the study "Those who are more desirable will get more quickly out of trouble than those who aren't" Beautiful here doesn't imply you're nice because everybody should be desirable. Don't just wake up and start doing the TikTok video.

The more time you spend having your brief musically or TikTok video look more beautiful the more people may enjoy it and retweet it and these people that follow you. That person who now has more than one million followers said to me, "I follow those people I consider more interesting and from whom I hope I will know"

2. WORKS WITH CELEBRITY TikTok USERS: It is a super-easy way to make TikTok popular. A person who has 1 million followers while collaborating with a TikTok consumer with 500 K followers is likely to gain everyone from this partnership. It is a specific characteristic known as "Mutual Beneficial" in humans, indicating that all are in the win-win scenario, neither one is risking something. Yeah, consider discovering others that create videos in the same niche as you do, and the odds of having more fans like yours can improve 10 times. Where to consider the customers of Popular TikTok? Really difficult issue. No. Join them, give them a post on Tik-Tok, pursue them even the other social networks, submit them the letter. Pro-

TIP: When certain popular users are advertising a conference or heading to a special function, seek to travel there and contact them. Ask them for a fast and short picture, and hope they don't mind working with you.

PHASE 2: BE ON THE TIKTOK SUPER ACTIVE.

If you're a TikTok person and want to go viral then to win the competition you need to reveal something lighter, more regular, and clearer than the others. Research has shown that low-profile individuals aren't as valued as others who are consistently hyperactive and constantly. Hyperactive accounts seem to get overloaded rather than regular ones. Usually, the development of continuous material coincides with hyperactivity. Constant content creation makes for higher chances of viral behavior on TikTok. The explanation for this is that on TikTok you don't realize precisely what Viral would go for. The creation of a broad variety of material also offers you further chances to go viral. If you make awesome material, your whole feed will continue to go viral on TikTok after one video goes viral. So, if you want to become popular for TikTok, then you need to hear your voice.

3. ATTACH ANNOTATIONS TO THE VIDEO(S).

Why Tags are important to Your TikTok Videos, here are some of the explanations why Tags should be included in your Videos: 1. Tags have the articles flaring. 2. People will find it quickly. 3. Any tags are fashionable, and if you add them then that means your videos would have more scope. 4. Simple to locate your videos on Web. 5. You should design your own logos and turn them into a niche. More and more people are going to be searching for it. 6. You may also create videos on famous topics, and use certain topics when uploading. For instance tag #TikTokGirl where only girls upload video in this folder.

Tag plays a key role in every social network, by taking the example of Twitter. How many users the tweet can reach depends on "What kind of tags you've used" And on Instagram, you attach tags depending on what's going on in the photo you're posting for. Seek to locate Tags are more and more people searching for them and hope that more people can find you.

4. SAY A AMUSING STOREY: What makes humans different from other species is sharing tales. The more tales you have the better you'll learn about issues, and the quicker you'll be able to affect others. Try telling a funny story because TikTok only requires you to post 15 seconds of video, but if you're a pretty great storyteller, you can easily relay your message in 15 seconds. Seek to stay on the Target and schedule things accordingly. Write a script and the times in your body that you must experience throughout the film. Get it humorous and succinct. Most users come using the Internet for both amusement and intelligence purposes. You're reading this post because you need more details on making TikTok big, but an individual watching Humorous Cat Videos is more interested in having entertainment. That is the entire idea behind why the Internet continues to function.

5. USING THE 'ABOUT YOU' TAB THE 'FOR YOU' tab is TikTok's main page allowing you to discover different artists and videos that match your taste. If you are sufficiently involved and frequently post quality material, then you are likely to make it to the website and be promoted for free.

6. USING OTHER CHANNELS TO YOUR BENEFIT. This is something most YouTubers do because doing Quest as a Vlogger is challenging for you, so most YouTubers are attempting to post their Vlogs videos on Facebook and other social networking sites. This brings them access to their target market and raises their impressions on YouTube and subscribers. The same principle can be used when marketing your TikTok profile and images. Seek to create a full package of your TikTok videos and upload it to YouTube, have a connection to your TikTok Profile in the title, which will enable people to identify you quickly and follow you without any hard work.

**Connect other social networking accounts to your TikTok, so that your peers and associates will quickly locate you on the web.

* Advertise the ads by sites on certain websites.

PHASE 3: ENGAGE IN CONTESTS & TOURNAMENTS ON VIRAL TIKTOK.

We can never overemphasize the value of competing in viral TikTok challenges & competitions. The app is typically popularly recognized every week for offering fresh, creative challenges. Viral challenges frequently include dancing or singing to a famous song, and many people enjoy watching TikTok's video of these trending challenges.

1. Many times these TikTok viral tests are flagship competitions. This helps you to not only create some interest from the TikTok community but also from the TikTok Company Community on your page. For starters, the Chipotle-started #guacdance competition generated a huge sensation around the viral sound byte. Though encouraging other TikTok influencers still to profit from the brand's potential sponsorships. So, to have your account noticed by a wide range of TikTok users, you should use these emerging TikTok challenges. A viral challenge will inspire you to further pursue a certain music genre or topic and build a readily recognizable look that will broaden your fanbase. Just below is a snapshot of several influencers on TikTok during the Viral Lipstick Contest!

2. Watch videos to get motivation There's not one form of video on TikTok that works well. You can notice everything from extremely crafted, put-together artsy images to Vine-reminiscent lowest effort photos. But, since the device has no clear feeds of interest, you'll need to cater to a wide audience. That normally involves planning an unlikely surprise or recording something insane or describing something that might blow the mind. Some people exhibit incredi-

bly stunning things (amazing weather, sexy men, or amazing experiences), and other TikTokers specialize in #hacks or realistic lifestyle images. The more time you spend on TikTok, the more themes you begin to find and get ideas for your own ventures. We started a spreadsheet where we started to discuss concepts for images. Any of our ideas include: * Show how to use Kapwing for basic tasks using a "screencast "- style video. * Use Kapwing on a tablet inside the vehicle. * Introduce Workplace men. * Do a demo wearing Kapwing swag on dance step. A Kapwinger-Peter-shows off his amazing pen-spinning abilities in one of our most popular photos. We arranged the video to show his talents at the end, to make things more unpredictable and shocking.

3. Upload videos external to TikTok. One way to stay out on TikTok is to use methods for video editing that are not feasible in the device, such as combining with a portion of a YouTube video or inserting subtitles. You can use Kapwing's Studio to create 9:16 collages and easily edit vertical videos online, then upload those videos to the web. We render almost all of our TikTok videos in a collaborative Digital Marketing Workspace on Kapwing and then post them to the TikTok page.

HOW TO EARN MONEY ON TIKTOK.

———————— ◆ ◇ ◆ ————————

#1 CREATE AND SELL TikTok ACCOUNTS.

That has become one of TikTok's most common and effective ways to make money. People create deposits, then sell them later. This is a legal place to earn profits. Its concept parallels what has trended on Instagram lately. What you do is find a place and create a profile around it. With TikTok, you build exclusive and innovative content around the market when you settle on a market. Verify that you produce engaging material that consumers would like to see and participate in. The aim is to use positive material to achieve full views and followers. Material that goes viral and that catches the imagination of the individual who will be the perfect client for this page. This definition is increasingly prevalent in the area of e-commerce and product space. And if you don't have a company to play with, promote and build content around; you can always generate content for a certain market and people can find you as long as your work goes viral. You may even create an account and then reach out to brands and companies to offer them your profile. Subsequently, such companies will leverage an already defined image to advertise and promote their commodity to a wide range of prospective clients. So, if you're fantastic at TikTok and you can build viral content then don't be scared to reach out to brands and sell your profile at a reasonable price!

#2 BE THE 'INFLUENT'

It is simpler to tell than done, but it can help you earn money by being an "influencer" on TikTok. While there are several various concoctions in this language and it is believed that everybody in today's society may be an "influencer." But the fact is, it's not easy to have the ability to manipulate and inspire your followers through the strength of your posts. When you are an "Influencer" in the true meaning of the term, you have the trust of the people who follow you and the power to persuade them to make any move or make a purchase. The skill is precisely what you can cash out with TikTok to make profits. You will gain influencer deals and work on making money from various companies. Brands are charging you to produce content for them and you are acting as the conduit to bind the company to hundreds of followers. You were still making material, why not make it for profits!

#3 BECOME "MANAGER OF INFLUENCER"

That's a perfect way to make money with TikTok, too. Being a TikTok influencer leaves you with not enough time and resources to even do the administrative duties. You should concentrate on making meaningful material, and think about nothing else. Hiring a boss is wiser; a boss who should be willing to take control of the jobs, obligations, and serve as supervisor. If you can be a manager then you can work with an influencer from TikTok and earn some income. You must handle all the correspondence between the companies and the influencer. It'll be your responsibility to build the deal, oversee the process, and ensure that all targets and deliverables are achieved. TikTok often provides influencer services that still pay a premium and if marketers and an influencer choose to stop the additional cost, they will private recruit a middle guy so that's what you will become and earn money with TikTok.

#4 THE FORUM FOR TikTok ADVERTISING.

TikTok also provides the right to view advertisements much like other social networking sites. You may also register with the TikTok ad platform and show your advertising if you operate a company or have a product or service to advertise. The fact that TikTok has over 500 million active users offers you a huge probability of being able to market and making revenue off your goods. #5 Touch. Finally, you will give many ambitious and fresh citizens on TikTok your professional opinion and useful pieces of advice. You would need to develop yourself as a popular TikTok star first to provide consulting services. When you can build material that is consumed by millions of viewers, and thousands of regular users support you; people will be interested in learning the secret recipe. You will teach and direct, and fee, new and aspiring TikTok influencers. Often, if anyone breaks an offer through your platform or guidance you can even get a cut. So, if you have earned a reputation through hard work and dedication; you can cash it out quickly!

#5. GIFTING

Before TikTok's life, Musical.ly was a live streaming website that was popular among humans. Musical.ly changed its name to TikTok, but then its live streaming (aka Go Live) apps are still common. You need at least 1,000 subscribers if you choose to live-stream. A TikTok app can conveniently live-stream and connect with thousands of users by messaging and communicating directly. Your viewers can even contribute coins (a virtual currency that can be bought from anyone inside the device through face recognition or fingerprint identification). Throughout the live-stream, the coins purchased will then be given to the influencer. TikTok does not officially announce coin pricing for each zone, but any registered consumer can then easily test the app's modified cost. Only go to "privacy and preferences," press "wallet," then "recharge." The smallest bundle in the United States is valued at 99 cents per 100 coins. When you have collected enough of these coins, you will raise 50 percent of the coins, exchange them for actual dollars, and then remove the matching dollar wallet. The remaining 50 percent is divided between the (depending on the platform) App Store / Google Play and TikTok.

#6. PARTNERSHIPS AND BRAND.

On TikTok, another way to raise money is by competitions and celebrity collaborations. That will be done as businesses and brands allow you to take part in music concerts, activities, or conventions as a special guest. Generally, the companies compensate you for appearing on stage (singing or dancing), endorsing a company, or simply attracting their fans. While the earnings rely on multiple variables such as the events demanded by the brand before, after, and after the case, a TikTok influencer's impact, and whether or not the brand is paying other expenditures such as flight and hotel.

#7 PROMOTING CROSS To All SOCIAL MEDIA NETWORKS.

Some of the social networking influencers you see now are still contacting their fans on their networks. If you already have an impact on other social networking sites, such as Instagram, YouTube, or Twitter, you will use your popularity on TikTok to support your other projects. In that way, you will be willing to make better use of your followers and maximize the number of views and comments for your other work as well. Which offers you lots of cross-promotional incentives. For starters, by spreading it through all the social networks, you will create an audience for a potentially live stream. You can also make highlight videos on TikTok and then add them to your YouTube channel later. Ordinary citizens regularly use three social networking devices, one of which may be TikTok. But several people don't use TikTok. You'll be able to broaden the potential reach by cross-promoting the TikTok events and merchandising on other social networking networks. This will also impact the future demand for purchases.

HOW TO CROSS TikTok HELP.

Below are some of the easiest places for other social networking networks to cross-promote away from TikTok:

* Use the same handles for all social media sites.

* Sure both channels are tested periodically.

* Engage on both channels for the viewer.

**Always post on social networking networks important, unique and fresh material.

* At the end of the TikTok videos, put social networking sites in.

1. HASHTAG THREATS AND ALLIANCES.

Hashtag competitions were a trend on TikTok where people shared related content through users. This is outstanding publicity and promotional space. As said earlier, partnering with influencers and celebrities on TikTok is also an important communication tool. TikTok has been a stable site with a wide base of users drawing numerous promotions and business players against it, rendering it an outstanding forum for earning revenue.

2. BRAND PERMITS.

Some of TikTok's most popular ways of earning money is by label endorsements. Because of TikTok's enormous presence, numerous brands and celebrities are using the site for promotional and advertisement purposes. This can be used to one's benefit in creating income through proper content production and successful techniques.

* Create your personalized profile and personality on the App.

* The key goal of the efforts will be to achieve the highest amount of followers.

**Create online material specifically that impresses viewers to the point that it becomes viral.

* Trend themes and songs are selected to produce unique and popular material.

**Link your other social networking accounts to Instagram, Facebook, and YouTube for a broader variety and better exposure to your posts, and raise followers.

* Increase your exposure with correct keyword tactics to increase the organic search traffic.

* Collaborate with other influencers and celebrities to make the brand and profile more famous and attentive.

* Once you have a sufficient amount of fans, you'll be contacted by endorsing joint products and partnerships, adding to profits.

INSTAGRAM.

———————— ◆◇◆ ————————

Instagram is a social networking web platform that posts images and videos. It was developed for smartphone users with the goal that consumers would take photographs on their smartphone devices and then post the pictures via the Instagram app "instantly." The aim is, like most social networking platforms, to associate users with friends, families, coworkers, and other users of common interests. The platform is focused mainly visually, with an emphasis on big, artistic pictures. Instagram now provides a range of filters that enable users to tweak and optimize their posts for optimum appeal with both images and videos. Instagram was bought by Facebook in 2012, catapulting it to the pinnacle of success of social media. Although it had been effective on its own previous to the purchase of Facebook, Facebook offered funding and site expansion capabilities. Nearly exactly one year after the Facebook contract, Instagram hit 150 million active monthly users on the benchmark. This is such an achievement that Instagram hit the amount faster than Facebook, Pinterest, Twitter, and LinkedIn! Google+ is the only platform that has reached the goal quicker than Instagram. The site's success continues to grow and it continues to attract more new users every day. The main audience was younger consumers in the 14-25 range when the platform was first released. Unfortunately, several people also think this is the case. But with more than 150 million active monthly users, I assure you the demographics have significantly grown! Instagram is popular with several age groups, and countless companies and industries. With over 60 percent of users outside the US, Instagram's global population continues to expand. Instagram is now a pioneer in social networking activity whether for personal usage or corporate marketing purposes!

HOW TO GET INSTAGRAM AND SET UP.

1. CHOOSE YOUR PHONE. Instagram is a Software for smart devices. You can not sign in on your machine (although after it is working you can enter your account). Upload the Instagram software to the App Store, Google Play, or Marketplace. Create no concerns, it's safe.

2. SAVE THE PASSWORD. After installing you will be asked to register or sign in until you launch the device. Whether this is the first time you have reported, you need to. Select this option, and enter your username and password. The symbol should transform green or red as you type your username in. If it is orange, then you're good to go. When it turns dark, someone else uses the account and you'll have to pick something new. *

Success Tip: Use a coherent username! Use something you'll recognize your friends, family, audience, customers, and fans. I suggest that you use the same name for your Twitter account. Instagram does not make looking for users very convenient, but having a name the target knows improves the likelihood of being noticed by them. Stop using the name's odd or jumbled combinations-it can render you hard to identify. To add a picture, click on the "Pic" button to show your profile photo. You may opt to upload a Facebook photo, take a screenshot, or upload an image from your phone collection. I strongly recommend using the same picture profile you have on other websites. Often you want people to approach you and know you instantly. Citizens want uniformity! Complete your profile details like your name, email address, and phone number (optional phone number). You can fill in this manually, or you can opt to fill in this detail automatically depending on your Facebook profile.

* **Progress Tip:** If you are using Instagram for your company profile, I will suggest that you fill in this detail manually. If you want to auto-fill in Facebook, your details would be inserted and will annoy the viewers whether they know you as a business name. Using your full name or company name (no matter how badly you like to be recognized). That is the name that will feature in the profile and searches below the username, etc. When such fields have been filled in, press Log.

3. SEE MATES. Facebook should seek to support you locate mates use Facebook now. You'll be asked to search already active Facebook mates. You may opt to miss the move too. Nevertheless, if you decide to do so, go ahead and press on the friends tab on Facebook. A pop-up should show up telling you if you want to post your Facebook interests before you can start. Through agreeing, every picture you want can feature on your Facebook page, and any picture you share on Instagram. If you're an involved Instagrammer you that be annoying your Facebook mates with all of your posts. At this point, you can choose "no" and then choose Facebook friends to link to. Each of your Instagram Facebook contacts should pop up next to their names with the "Join" keys. Go down the list and press "follow" on whomever you want. When a person has their profile set to "Public," follow them may only be "requested." The consumer always must accept your followup before their posts appear on your list. When you're done press on "Prev." Instagram would then allow you to access your smartphone to locate contacts. To do so, you'll need to grant Instagram permission to transfer details regarding your address book to their servers (using a protected connection). You may either opt to accept this, based on your faith and interest in privacy, or you can miss this phase. So because you still haven't met enough people to link to quite yet, Instagram will now recommend users to join you. You can click through this list and join any of these individuals you choose.

* Performance Tip: Contrary to recommended applications, there are pros and cons. Following these very popular pages, you'll get fantastic examples of what goes best on Instagram and give you suggestions on what kinds of images and hashtags to use. Chances are, though, that such people do not obey you back and will not communicate sincerely with you. Those users may or may not help you, based on your Instagram approach. Just so you know, when I began (for educational purposes) I wanted to follow some of these pages, but later I unfolded them and preferred to concentrate my feed and attention on more important connections.

4. PROFILE UPDATE. You will now fill in your profile details and set up your profile settings once you're signed. At the bottom of the device, click on the right-most button (it looks like a business card or phone address). Your profile would inform you how many updates you have posted (photos and videos), how many friends you have and how many accounts you follow. There's an arrow right below these stats to change your profile. Click this field to fill in details regarding your page. It is the only way you'll add a clickable URL on Instagram. If you use Instagram for work, please fill in the URL of your company website. Otherwise, you should insert the URL of your Facebook account or some other connection to the social networking platform. Or you might only leave this open. Enter a brief bio that describes you or your company. Seek to hold the knowledge in sync with what you are doing on other pages. You've got 150 characters to convince the universe who you are, so do well!

* Tip for success: Have a certain trait in your profile, just like certain pages. Don't find this so dull or stuffy. Tell them who you are, what you are doing, and whether you are "you" You have the opportunity on this computer to render your posts private too. You'll see a tiny box (currently NOT checked), indicating that the posts are available. Whether you are using Instagram for personal usage, and want to keep your photos private, check the privacy tab. Whether you are using Instagram for enterprise or free networking, though, I suggest that you leave this unregulated! Whether you're doing this for company or promotions, much as on Facebook, you'll alienate and shame fans whether you lock the pictures to private. Make sure you click on "Save" after all the edits are completed.

5. SETTING YOUR INSTAGRAM NETWORKING PARAMETERS

helps you to connect your content with other social media platforms. During the collection of contacts, if you chose not to link with Facebook, you may always be linked to Facebook so that is just for convenience sharing. You may manually opt to distribute post uploads on any mixture of these other platforms by linking the other social networking pages without needing to re-enter the username credentials each time. Tap on the 3 tiny dots at the top right of your page (on your profile photo) to link your other social networking pages to Instagram, then tap on "Sharing Settings." You will note that this searches Twitter. Clicking on the Facebook link (should include an arrow to open another tab), would open another website. When from the stage of friends you chose not to post likes, you may find that the "Likes" box is unchecked. When you'd like to show all of your Facebook posting operations, check this page. Other accounts may be connected like Twitter, Foursquare, and Flickr. To connect the accounts, check the box for the respective site and fill in your login credentials. Uncheck the account name if you want to unlink some accounts. You should get a pop-up to indicate you want certain accounts to be unlinked.

6. TAKE PICTURES (AND SOME VIDEOS)! Images on Instagram are all black. Both articles are cropped in this square format to blend in. Images in the feed are set to 612 x 612 pixels. Instagram can, therefore, support a maximum resolution of 2048 x2048 (depending on your device). You have two photo-taking choices.

* First, if you want to take images directly from Instagram, press the big camera icon in the middle of the toolbar at the left. Then make sure you've selected the blue camera icon-this is to take pictures. Or you can only right-click the camera icon to take screenshots. The advantage of taking photos directly from Instagram is that your viewing field is set to the square size allowed for photos from Instagram. This means you keep the focus on your items within the picture sector.

* Second you will use your standard camera feature to take images. You may upload it to Instagram after you've taken the shot. The benefit of taking pictures from your phone is you have more editability within the app of your device. Nonetheless, note that your Instagram images should be cut to a square and you won't have anything in your initial picture frame.

ETIQUETTE Of INSTAGRAM.

As a "virtual" web platform, Instagram has several tags to remember.

1. People follow.

When you are about to follow somebody on Instagram, just don't add them and click their new post. Go via their list as well as via other entries. Report on at least one of the photos. You might also claim this article encouraged you to join them. Reaching out to them like that would create a clear bond from the beginning and as a result, they will always follow you back. Keep the relationship through by continuing to like and comment on further future posts. Furthermore, following a bunch of other people is not appropriate to get them to support you and then turn around and unfollow them. That's not how you let an audience develop! Join users you are not only involved in creating likes.

2. Sharing Photos.

When Instagram's success grows, I'm seeing more and more users take the "simple" path to picture sharing. Instagram is all about sharing images of your own! Instagram aims to share images instantly-right when you're getting them to your computer. Hence the word "insta!" I realize we could not exchange them immediately at all. In reality, I always suggest that you wait and spread your posts out. And I know several photographers who use their DSLR cameras to capture pictures and then format them after the event for Instagram upload. I'm fine about these two activities. I'm not ok with Instagrammers using pictures from other users, or photos they found on Google, however. Photos on Instagram should be a representation of you! Use pictures of other individuals is not a representation of yourself. Most of us get used to sharing inspiring quotes or seasonal photos that we find in searches. On Twitter, and some of the other pages, it is incredibly popular. I get it, it's better than our production. And sometimes we hear something that really resonates well and we want to express it. But this activity is not really about Instagram. If you want to share an inspirational quote, just place it on your own image! Take a few extra minutes to pick a decent screenshot from your album, add text to the quotation, and post the optimized image to your Instagram page afterward. There are many apps that you can use, attaching text to pictures. However, you should note that many Instagrammers are highly careful about their copyrights. When they catch you using one of their pictures without acknowledgment or acknowledgment they can rat you out. Trust me when I tell you that's not the image you want Instagram to make! Also, you should consider the frequency with which you share Instagram posts. No one wants to go through their feed and see 25 pictures from you, one immediately after another. Place the images to make sure the photographs from other users fill the space behind yours. This will not only keep your images alive throughout the day(s) but also through your focus on each photograph. When you post 10 photos in a series, the second or third one, people would pause and like and reflect. If you spread them out and hold them fresh, though, on each article you are more likely to start to get likes on comments in higher proportions. Share just the right photos for your viewers, too. Only because you've got 3 separate views from the birthday cake doesn't suggest you ought to reveal any of them. Select the best one, and post it.

3. Of Instagram, get results.

Now that you're comfortable with using Instagram, you need to get out there and get tests! Below are a few fast ideas to help you improve engagement and outcomes.

- Add more content-people don't want selfish accounts to imitate. Write regularly!

- Post quality content – people aren't going to connect as often if any of the articles are blurred or badly written.

- Use filters-different filters of viewers create different emotions. Use these for your good

- Use hashtags-see your tweets!

- Build your following – more fans means more people will want your content.

- Be involved!

- Allow more available for Snapchat! You go back, then! You're all ready to get engaged and start getting progress on Instagram!

TikTok VS. INSTAGRAM.

Several social networking sites come up every day, but they don't all have the potential to become famous and go viral. Instagram performed so well and it easily had a lot of followers from all over the planet that it expanded more than Facebook, which was used before Instagram. TikTok is a new social network after Instagram which has shocked people with its development and strong download numbers. Through being a common TikTok client, several people compare these two sites to better learn Instagram and TikTok to select which one to use and invest more time on. You've certainly noticed a lot of teens and young people who spend a lot of time on their mobile phones, TikTok might be one of the sites they spend time on.

TikTok.

TikTok is a freshly described, related program to Dubsmash, but entirely separate from other channels. TikTok, known in China as Douyin, is a forum for sharing and video-making about a particular tune. TikTok revealed in June 2018 that it has crossed 500 million monthly active users spanning 150 nations, this is the first device since WeChat to go viral in a short period. TikTok suits all ages; you can notice there some videos like humor, music, animals, sports, food, vlog, etc. But the numbers indicate that most TikTok users are mainly young adults, adolescents, and teenagers who film themselves when dancing with a famous album. Therefore, we may say that most TikTok users are generation Z people. Figures indicate that 8.2 million TikTok people are girls and women who are higher than 6.1 million male users. Up to 15 seconds of TikTok videos can be filmed with multiple effects, filters, and stickers that help you enhance the images. In getting the caption alternative, TikTok is close to Instagram but it's restricted to 100 characters. It seems like influencers are now involved in using TikTok to encourage their fans to join them on TikTok as well on Twitter, Snapchat, Facebook, etc. E.g., Sssniperwolf, who is a popular Instagram video gamer, has been urging her followers to watch her videos on TikTok and follow her on the app.

ARE HASHTAGS IMPORTANT ON TikTok?.

Believe it or not, TikTok hashtags play a significant part, more so than Instagram! Hashtags are known on TikTok as useful, realistic concepts and help you get more attention and likes. Sharing images on TikTok is a major error, without utilizing hashtags! Using popular hashtags enables your videos to be seen and lead your TikTok followers to slowly increase in number. Below we've gathered a list of common hashtags on Instagram and TikTok: Also, you can notice that some hashtags can be famous in a span and then it will be forgotten after a few days, including challenging hashtags; you may recall the last viral Instagram challenge that was the Instagram bottle cap challenge, some hashtags including #bottlecap, #bottlecapchallenge, #challenge.

Are there any advertisements on both TikTok and Instagram? (Models on revenue).

Instagram and TikTok have very specific business models; Instagram's business is focused on its advertising displayed to users on their Instagram feed and stories centered on user age, location, interests, etc. If you're a Tik-Tok regular, you might have found that there's no advertisement on TikTok, which I think might be the key reason it's been so famous around the world. Having commercials everywhere these days on mobile phones as we browse the internet, on social media, on street signs, on stores, etc. will eventually render us sick of having tons of advertising surrounding them and maybe search for a way to just have fun without seeing commercials. Revenue from TikTok is focused on in-app transactions by consumers, such as promotional gifts and emojis. TikTok made $3.5 million in in-app sales in only one month of October 2018. If you are involved in learning TikTok Figures, we have compiled some of them here:

* TikTok has been downloaded more than 660 M times in 2018.

* TikTok is more common with Android, compared to iOS.

* Over 500 million people globally use TikTok every month

* 26.5 million of the 500 million active monthly users are from the U.S.

* TikTok user base is primarily based in India with 43 percent of all users.

**66 percent of consumers were under the age of 30.

* Consumers usually average around 52 minutes a day with the device.

**80% of TikTok sessions run on Android apps.

**In-app sales rose year-over-year by 275 percent.

* 29 percent of monthly TikTok users are available hourly.

* TikTok has over 685.7 million impressions on the #RaindropChallenge.

**Jimmy Fallon's #TumbleweedChallenge produced 8,000 videos in seven days, with over 9 million views.

* Over 5 million #InMyFeelings challenge videos are accessible on TikTok as opposed to 1.7 million on Instagram.

TikTok IS THE ANTI-INSTAGRAM AND COMPANIES ARE SEEKING TO CLONE IT.

TikTok, one of the most popular applications of the past decade, is leading the path to just about everyone in a world of simple content production. The massively successful social-networking video-sharing site is operated by ByteDance, a business established in 2012 headquartered in Beijing. Users build and upload lip-sync, humor, and talent videos in three to 60 seconds. According to Sensor Tower, by February 2019, TikTok had reached a cumulative 1.5 billion download from the Apple AAPL, -1.35 percent from the App Store and GOOG from Alphabet, + 1.56 percent from GOOGL, + 1.71 percent from Google Play, 123.8 million from the US. The website draws primarily a younger audience since two-thirds of the members are under 30 (about 60 percent of active monthly users in the U.S. are between the ages of 16 and 24)

1. FRIVOLOUS FUN. But how does TikTok work right? Content developers are taking and reinterpreting popular forms, such as videos, images, and songs, in their own way. Hundreds of designers pair a song with tongues, each applying their own spin to it. You may define the content exchanged through TikTok as mostly trivial, but users don't matter. They're having fun making it and don't seem offended by media attention. TikTok is either the reverse or a calculated spoof of what's on Instagram; its members go out of their way to ridicule the designs, high-profile quality standards, and originality of this particular website. If anything, most TikTok developers thoroughly accept the silliness, and therein lies their greatest strength: keeping the entry bar low. TikTok encourages everyone to rapidly step in and produce material, without the labor that reaches the refined output. Specific problems and video trends can be checked by hashtags (such as hashtags on Twitter TWTR, + 0.56 percent) and reflect what is happening on the web today. Taking part in these competitions not only offers web producers inspiration for future clips but also a feeling of belonging to a larger culture.

2. FACEBOOK TAKES Care. TikTok is a trend that has taken the planet by surprise and Facebook FB is starting to catch up by + 1.69 percent. In November 2018, the social networking company attempted to replicate TikTok, culminating in Lasso — a separate copycat device that struggled to gain major follow-ups. Following the failed effort, Facebook returned to its old practices of cloning related features and inserting them into the company's already widely-popular applications. That's how Snapchat (run by Snap Drop, -0.30 percent) was defeated in 2016 when Instagram cloned its hallmark app Tales. Reels was launched last November to Instagram users in Brazil — a live-music replay app that enables them to create 15-second long video clips utilizing a database album. Until introducing it elsewhere, Facebook needs to check Reels on markets that are not yet saturated with TikTok Having the code and correct features correctly is not the only problem. The key challenge remains as I described earlier: If the Instagram community will not accept the silliness brand of TikTok, Reels is not going to be a product that they choose to use. The group itself may prevent anyone from utilizing it, bullying, and harassing the producers of material who seek. Finally, an explosion of TikTok-like material on Instagram might alienate the current community who would consider the new format unpalatable to them.

3. EVERYONE'S A CONTENT Maker. But here's a larger picture. Tik-Tok offers us a glimpse into the future of social networking, one in which the least time is expended on becoming a content maker with a global success shot or at least a few laughs if they like. The trend is not unlike what occurred with the introduction of YouTube (now operated by Alphabet) to video content: formality, protocol, and high-quality standards previously seen on Television shows give way to spontaneity, informality, and intimate, often emotional, interactions with the viewer. Now the walls between content producers and content users are more collapsing thanks to TikTok and related social networks, blurring the gap between the two. TikTok is a turbulent culture that is constantly in flux — unpredictable, childish, and sometimes uncouth — but real as well.

So, which one do you want — TikTok or Instagram?

SOCIAL MEDIA.

———————— ◆ ◇ ◆ ————————

THE WORLD FOR SUCCESS MARKETING ON YOUTUBE, FACEBOOK, TWITTER, AND INSTAGRAM.

Many marketers see social networking ads as the next huge trend, a strong yet fleeting fad that needs to be manipulated whilst it's in the spotlight. To some, it is just a buzzword that has little real value and with it, there is a complex, steep learning curve. Regardless of the fast speed at which social networking has established its popularity, certain company owners regard this as a fleeting marketing activity, thus it is believed to be non-profitable. The estimates also reflect various results. HubSpot estimated that 92 percent of advertisers believed that social media marketing was essential for their company in 2014, with 80 percent suggesting that attempts to promote social networking also boosted traffic to their websites. According to Social Media Examiner, 97 percent of advertisers engage in social media marketing, but 85 percent of participants are not aware which social media marketing strategies are the best to use, and how they should start marketing on social media. This indicates that social media marketing has tremendous potential for revenue growth, but there is a lack of awareness among entrepreneurs as to how to achieve such results. Until we move into how you can effectively inject yourself into the social media marketing environment, let's discuss how social media marketing will help you and your company.

1. INCREASES BRAND RECOGNITION.

This is of tremendous importance to the chance a company owner has to syndicate their content and through their exposure to their future buyers and partners, as well as to their existing ones. Social networking networks are only a different platform for the company to express its opinion and raise the visibility of its product and service. This is important for your company as it allows your company more open to potential clients and buyers, and also allows you more recognized and recognizable to others who have previously done business with you. E.g., regular Twitter users can learn about your business for the first time only after their newsfeed has stumbled upon it. Maybe an otherwise apathetic customer may become more familiar with your company and brand after having seen your appearance on many different networks.

2. IMPROVES LOYALTY TO THE COMPANY.

Brands who connect with their social networking platforms have higher consumer satisfaction ratings. Companies can take advantage of the opportunities offered by the social network when it comes to communicating with an audience. A transparent and realistic approach for social networking appears to be successful in keeping customers loyal to a company.

3. MORE CHANCES TO CONVERT.

Each message you placed on social networking networks is an incentive to attract a consumer or company. When you create follow-ups, you obtain exposure to existing clients, old clients, and potential consumers at the same time. You may also communicate with them all concurrently. Any photograph, blog post, photo, or message you want to share is an invitation for others to respond to what you've shared, and any response will contribute to visitors to the web, and finally conversions. Not all social networking interactions with your company can result in a conversion, but every successful communication can improve the likelihood of a future conversion. And if the click-through performance is small, the sheer amount of opportunities you have is a game-changer.

4. SUPERIOR TRANSFER SPEEDS.

In a few different forms, social network ads can carry in a better conversion rate. The most significant approach is via the dimension of humanization. Once you connect with social networking sites the name is more humanized. Social networking is a platform that businesses will behave as customers do, and that's important because consumers are doing business with other individuals, not just a company. Furthermore, statistics indicate that social networking has a similar incidence of one hundred percent higher initial interaction than outbound ads, so a larger percentage of social network fans continue to improve the brand's reputation so confidence. Regardless of that, even creating your following on social networking sites increases the existing traffic conversion levels. Furthermore, the brand can look more trustworthy for potential consumers. If you connect on Twitter or other social networking sites with big influencers, your measurable scope for authority can grow drastically. People want to associate with businesses that they find to be the strongest in a specific sector or niche. Fifth Inbound Traffic Improved. When you will not have a social networking presence, the inbound traffic would be restricted to users who are already acquainted with your business and persons that are looking for keywords on search engines that you are listed with. Any social networking profile you have is another route that leads back to your site and every article you make, click, tweet or connect, is another way for a potential user to engage with you. The more quality content you get on social networking sites, the more inbound visitors you'll receive, and the more visitors you'll get will mean more leads, which would inevitably contribute to more sales.

5. PUBLICITY EXPENSES REDUCED.

84 percent of companies found, according to a survey undertaken by Hub-Spot, that just six hours of work a week was enough to generate an improved amount of traffic on their pages. With networks as big as social networking sites, six hours isn't a massive commitment. When you can lend only one hour a day to build content and sharing techniques, you'll almost certainly begin to see the benefits of your efforts. Only paying advertisement is relatively inexpensive via Twitter and Facebook, depending on the priorities. Start low, and don't have to think about going through the estimate. When you have a clearer understanding of what you should do on these sites, you will increase the expenditure as well as increase the sales that you have.

6. INCREASE IN ENGINE PERFORMANCE SCORES.

SEO is the best way to catch specific traffic from the search engines, but there are still variations in the requirements to stay on top. It's no longer enough for you to refresh your blog regularly, ensuring that structured title tags and Meta details are filled in and delivery links lead back to your web. Search engines such as Google and Bing may be measuring their results utilizing the involvement of social networking as a major factor as strong marketers prefer to utilize social media. And being prominent on social media might serve as a brand indicator to a search engine that your company is a true, trustworthy, and reputable one. It suggests that it could be important to have a good profile on social media should you plan to compete with a specified keyword.

7. BETTER SERVICES FOR CONSUMERS.

Social networking is at its heart a medium of contact, including phone calls and emails. Any user experience you have on social media is an opportunity to demonstrate your quality of customer support to the public and it is an opportunity to strengthen your partnership with your consumers. For example, if anyone on Facebook wanted to complain regarding a product, you might answer the issue, personally apologize to them and take steps to remedy the problem. And, if anyone praises you, you may like to ask them for any complimentary items and suggest them. It's the intimate connection that tells the customers that you truly feel for them.

8. BETTER CONSUMER SENSITIVITY.

Social networking offers the business the chance to learn some useful insights into what attracts future consumers and how they behave in a social environment. For example, you may track comments and see what people specifically say about your company, or look for comments aimed at your industry. You should break the content into the topic-based lists to see what types of content attract the most attention from consumers, and then generate more of that kind of content. You can calculate the sales you are getting based on the numerous promotions shared on different social media sites and find the right mix to generate revenue for your company. If you're a company, there are several perks of being on social media, but all of those advantages boil down of one aspect – you get more publicity for your company, which turns into more profits. Your bottom line would be thanked for putting a little bit of time and money into your work on social networking.

THE SOCIAL MEDIA PROGRAM MARKETING, WHY DO YOU NEED ONE.

——— ◆◇◆ ———

Social media marketing strategies provide in-depth descriptions of all things you intend to do by keeping your company successful on social media. Without a concrete strategy, social networking marketing sounds like a futile mission, and without focus, the capacity for growth is suffering greatly. While social media might have seemed like the Wild West of a brand's marketing efforts, the promotional medium has matured to the point where it offers companies tangible, true, and observable impacts on the income of their company. Social networking management needs to operate in tandem with the remainder of the corporate plan to ensure the brand's strategic targets are achieved. There are six steps toward developing a communication campaign for social networking, which we will discuss throughout the remainder of this essay. Note, a social media strategy is just like any other aspect of your business plan, ensuring that specifics are needed to affect your company.

PHASE 1: HAVE AN IMPRESSION ON YOUR SOCIAL NETWORKING TARGETS.

Much like every other campaign strategy, establishing goals is the first move toward a successful one. Specifying your targets allows you a straightforward path to calculate your marketing plan's performance, so it's a path you can keep track of the return on investment (ROI). Growing consumer satisfaction and rising revenue Raising client interest and future customer interaction with the business Growing access to a website Enhancing customer support division Increasing the number of followers or supporters, which can raise the number of followers or supporters. It's just like anything else in life to create goals for a social media marketing campaign – you don't want to start so wide with a target, because that would imply you've spread your money too thinly and you risk not achieving your main goal. One of the easiest ways to set a target is to build a SMART objective, whether it's personal or business-related. If you've previously read about these, it's because the Clever targets are just that smart, because they work. If you don't recognize the acronym SMART, it means General, Measurable, Attainable, Realistic, and Timely. Let's have a deeper look at each letter if you don't know about this type of target setting or need a refresher.

* Determined. There's no sense in being ambiguous regarding the expectations that you set. Then you're not going to have a specific goal at which you shoot. And let's get precise. For example: Raise website visits to our company blog leveraging links posted on social networking accounts including Facebook and Twitter twice a week;

* Metaphorical. If you want to learn if your social media marketing strategy and subsequent actions are making money for your business or increasing exposure to potential customers or consumers, then you have to reach measurable goals. Vague, unmeasurable objectives may cause you to see a slight improvement or aim at one, but a more precise tangible target than that. It could be something like a 20 percent boost website traffic to our company blog linked to my social media channels.

* Enabled. It is the number one error that companies and individuals create while setting a goal. We make it impossible to do because they want to do everything at once. There's no quick target click here. When you attempt to go so hard you can inevitably set up yourself for disappointment. Hence, question the ambitions but still make sure they are achievable. For example Increasing website visits from 1,000 unique visitors to 1,200 unique visitors to our client blog via social networking platforms by 20 percent.

**Related. Make sure your social networking targets are genuinely matched with the rest of your business goal, or you'll get irritated quickly. For example: attracting traffic to your blog would introduce readers to your free product guides and industry insights, and encourage them to get a subscription to guides and industry insights, and encourage them to get a subscription to your mailing list for more details and alerts that will, in effect, motivate them to buy goods and services from your company.

* On schedule. Ultimately, you need to establish a target timeline. Targets are open-ended without a timetable and don't allow you to establish specific targets along the road to reach a target. Timeframes help you be responsible, motivated, and less likely to wander from the road when it comes to executing a strategy. For example: By the end of the fourth quarter in 2020, we plan to increase our website traffic to our blog utilizing social media channels.

PHASE 2: SOCIAL MEDIA PROFILES CREAT
(OR SPRUCE UP OLD ONES).

You have nailed down your priorities and it's time to start building accounts that can impress your future clients and consumers. This one has a few mini moves to it. But let's continue with the first – finding out which social networking networks you will be entering.

WHAT SOCIAL NETWORKS TO JOIN.

Each social networking platform out there has unique facets of it. Which works on one social networking network won't function on another, so the key features of each network will differ considerably. Not every social networking network wants you to be involved! The trick is to concentrate on only one or two who will enable you to attain your marketing strategy for social networking best. Social networking viewers and trends are perhaps the most important aspect you ought to remember. You've already also got a decent understanding of where the customers like to hang out socially, but surveys such as Pew Research Center's The Demographics about Social Media Consumers offer more quantitative statistics on the five biggest social networks – Pinterest, Facebook, Snapchat, Instagram, and LinkedIn. Other things to remember include how much money you have to invest in social network ads, and what tools you have at your fingertips. It should help you find out which social network suits better with your company.

* Optimization of accounts in the social network. An up-to-date, full social networking profile should allow a strong first impression on your guests. It will demonstrate the integrity of the company, which will convince customers that you are ready for business. Refreshing profiles from time to time is a smart thing, but you must continue on the right foot.

* Upload profile pictures and cover images tailored to your social network profile.

* Complete the About and Introduction pages for each network, tailoring the document to the social networking community you've entered.

* Audit yourself and your peers. If you have already built a footprint on social networking platforms, the best moment to carry out an audit is the moment you prepare a marketing campaign. Audits guarantee that all the social network accounts are up-to-date, and provide you with visibility on how rivals work. Look through the following checklists to help you get going with a detailed analysis of your profiles and the profiles of your rivals.

* A summary of the service.

1. Find and take care of any page the organization has on social media, unofficial and official. To prevent misunderstanding, the accounts and fan pages set up by staff or supporters will be combined or purged.

2. Be sure that your profile and cover images are all up to date and in line with the identity of the business.

3. Update the Bios and About parts with recent messages and facts, use the tone and language ideally adapted to the social network you are using. Facebook for starters is more laid back than LinkedIn.

4. Take notice of the profile's followers and fan pages, and when the last action was reported. When one account appears to slip behind the others, even though you are still blogging, decide whether it will be worth your time to continue with that channel or if your energies will be more directed elsewhere.

* Profiles of rivals.

1. Find several social networking pages operated by rivals at your business, either from one network or from several networks.

2. Take notice about how often the websites of such organizations are modified with new content, what they are writing, and what kind of support the articles earn on average in views, favorites, and comments.

3. Write down the date and a total number of followers and loves their profile, which is a guide for you to figure out their progress relative to the development of the business at a later period.

4. Examine their product branding-user description, logo cover, and sound. Will they send a clear representation of the offerings of the business, the business, and the style of the company? Was it all that you would want to imitate, or do you prefer to step away?

PHASE 3: A LOT OF SPEECH BUILDING.

As in every type of communication, the way you talk to your customers or communicate with them has a huge effect on how they perceive your business and you. Product personality is a collection of associative and emotional characteristics related to a product or business name. Such factors can influence how people perceive a company, and how they communicate with a company. The characteristics of the company also mirror those of its intended customers. While you might still have a good sense of what the essence of your company looks like, the following series of questions should ensure that everybody on the team has a clear frame of reference to use.

* If your business or brand were an entity, what kind of personality would that have?

* If your company were a customer, what would their partnership be?

* Would they be like friends, teammates, professors, parents, etc.?

* Write down what the business is not, use adjectives.

* Are there corporations whose identities are close to your brand?

**Why are there related companies?

* What do you want consumers to see your brand or company?

After you've addressed these queries, you will have a clear sense of the sound your social networking ads should provide and you'll be gearing up to start producing and posting material, so let's look at phase four before you move into that.

PHASE 4: TECHNIQUE GENERATING A MESSAGE.

You may have the best-looking social networking page and the highest ideas in the world, but if you don't have a marketing schedule and a blogging policy, you will waste both of those efforts. Rather than plowing ahead without a plan, take some time to build a posting technique that will blow the competition out of the water right away. Remember the following points:

* What types of material would you write, and who would be accountable for producing such information? Photos are a requirement for most social

networking sites but video content is a core tool for the marketing campaigns of other businesses. Certain material types contain numbers, quotations, quizzes, comics, and many others.

* How much do you write, and at what times in the daytime? There's also a discussion going on about whether the right to publish is publishing pace and time of day. The fact is, not a one style suits all this answer. The response to that query is special to your company and your audience. How much you choose to share may rely on the field in which you operate, the capacity to create and curate successful material, the scope, and the social network you use. For a general rule, businesses will plan to publish one to two times a day on Facebook, five to six times a day on Twitter, and once a day on LinkedIn and Instagram. The time of day you post content can be decided by historical experience, whether by approaching your followers when they are more likely to be involved on social media, such as before morning work, after evening work, or at any point on the weekends.

* How would the site be marketed using both free and charged strategies? Without a committed, broad, and active audience, publishing an update and assuming it would be going well does not succeed for you in the long run. For exposure pressure in the fans' social networking channels, sharing the same material in various formats several days, as well as engaging them for paid promotions, will be a big part of the approach.

An ideal way to keep track of your growth, and when to update is to create a calendar of social networking posts. It will help you prepare ahead of time for weeks or months, and give you an indication of the material that you should share to social media. This will help keep you from posting incoherently and unexpectedly and will encourage you to incorporate patterns through your regular, monthly, and seasonal updates. Spontaneous messaging to social media also has its position, for example in reaction to breaking news or a problem in customer care that needs to be resolved instantly, so a content calendar is a solid idea towards the majority of the marketing campaign.

PHASE 5: EXPERIMENT AND EVALUATE.

When it comes to the effectiveness of social networking campaigns there is no silver bullet. Your business sends out the most updates, because the more you explore, the better you can figure out what material would fit well for your organization, the hours of the day are great for interaction operation, because how much you need to add new products. More critically, the attempt to compete socially will never be stagnant. You can do more workable stuff, but also be open to experimenting with different material, particularly if it's different for your business in the industry. Instead of wondering, using a monitoring method is the best way to learn what's going and what isn't. Sites like Twitter, Facebook, and Pinterest have built-in metrics that you can use to offer you a clear understanding of how your profile performs and expands, including post and account views, famous tweets, profiles for the crowd, and many more. You may want to think, however, a single monitoring device, such as Hootsuite, to have anything in one location. Another approach to evaluate your social media marketing plan's effectiveness is to use connection shorteners and keep track of the connection clicks, and the social portion of Google Analytics is a perfect resource to control the effect of social network marketing on your website.

* Structured approach to research. There are moments where the number of numbers and maps is daunting, and here's one way you can easily organize your tests on social media.

1. Choose what you intend to check for. Is it the pace at which your video posts engage? Will you receive references to the website? Your photos reaching? Only choose one.

2. Set one goal. Check the statistics on the element you have selected to check and take note of it after a certain time, a week, or a month. This will be the baseline for the following evaluation chapter.

3. Double-down, or seek fresh. Experiment with the posting strategy's modifications, and then review the target over another period to see whether success has decreased, changed, or remains the same. Adjust the technique to maximize it and make it a regular part of the marketing plan, based on the outcome. If it doesn't fit then again try something new.

4. Have you achieved your goal?

PHASE 6: PROCESS AUTOMATE, ENGAGE WITH FOLLOWERS, OR LISTEN.

The most beautiful thing about a comprehensive social media marketing strategy is that you can schedule the majority of your advertising plans in advance, and then you will use automated software to queue the material, post it, and deliver it precisely how the marketing plan has specified. Hootsuite, Post Planner, and Buffer are also fantastic checkout devices. Once you have optimized your publishing routine, you free up your energy to communicate with your community.

In a regular basis, you should set aside time to talk and connect with consumers who are interacting with your material, address queries, and thank people that have shared your articles, as well as successful search and native alerts, apps like Mention and Google Alerts give you reminders anytime someone has discussed your brand online, which encourages you to re-share or engage with the message.

If you have a social media communication strategy in motion, you become a lot more comfortable in selling your company via social media. You are much more positioned to meet social network marketing targets. Note these moves, build your campaign and you'll be well on the path to marketing success in social media!

TIPS ON FACEBOOK FOR MARKETING.

———— ◆ ◇ ◆ ————

As an advertising device, Facebook wins the success battle as a central factor among certain corporate communication campaigns. However, due to the durability of Facebook messages, you may notice that you are struggling all the time to come up with new material and fresh ideas for your business or brand profile. Although writing up some material, discovering some adorable photos, or sharing nonstop is enticing, approaching it with a technique would increase the chances of participating in meaningful consumer and audience conversations. The following suggestions will motivate you to step up your marketing activities.

* TIMING.

Because it depends on your target market, material, and priorities, you ought to carefully evaluate the pacing of your updates. Look at the target group, take care of their characteristics, and plan the articles as needed. For starters, if you approach busy mothers who are sitting at home, the best time to hit them would most definitely be different from targeting single bachelors. One effective approach to finding out what times function better is with some trial and error, but with a little more precision, there is another method to continue with. Research has also been done to decide which various kinds of users are online, so beginning posting on Thursdays and Fridays is a reasonable starting point, as these are the most popular days on Facebook. Commitment rates continue to decline by 3.5 percent below the Monday to

Wednesday average. Therefore, one in the afternoon is the best time to post for a share, and three is the best time to post for a button. Those are not the most common hours for posting on Facebook though. This is the post's timing that can show a spike in interest and not the common hours the audience would be writing.

* SNAPSHOTS.

You've most definitely seen this one a million times, but you can't stress more the advantages of attaching photos to the messages you place on Facebook. Images can get 84 percent more connection clicks and 53 percent more Facebook shares than the typical message. Below are a few useful ideas for Facebook photos.

1. Share real-life photos.

2. Using imagery for lifestyle rather than imagery for items.

3. Emphasis on the face of men.

4. Be violent.

5. Create galleries.

6. Encourage quick reaction.

7. For your favor, use nostalgia.

* CONTEST.

Customers want to have things for cheap. Everybody finds themselves to enjoy and connect with a sponsored Facebook account that they wouldn't have been conscious of until they had the opportunity to win anything. The excitement of maybe having it for free is one of the greatest rewards, which would most definitely cost your company very little due to the exposure the brand receives through the contest. The key reasons users on Facebook 'heart' products is so they can get a deal, coupon, or offer. Although the principle of growing interaction is strong, through the usage of Facebook competitions for companies, there are 7 clear returns on investments made.

1. It through the collection of followers.

2. This increases flow.

3. It produces content that is produced by the consumer.

4. It creates target views on the sector.

5. This raises and spreads the virality.

6. This engenders discussions.

7. It's making the email list rising.

* CROWDSOURCED RESPONSES.

A crowdsourcing consumer and viewer reviews for improving your Facebook participation is one of the advantages of holding Facebook contests. Crowdsourcing is a form of collective networking that is essential for campaigns on social platforms. The favorite subject of discussion for everyone is themselves, so appealing to Facebook fans to get feedback and suggestions about something is a perfect way to improve interaction. Tell your new Facebook followers a specific request, or using a questionnaire to ask them to decide on a topic, and you'll have a quick way to see just what your consumers and viewers want. Below are several tips for painless crowdsourcing to bring the best out of the public.

1. Using the queries to collect testimonials.

2. Gather feedback from your article.

3. Ask your fans to send pictures using their items from your store.

4. Host a picture contest and gather the brand's photos.

5. Run a race.

* POSTS TO BOOST.

While there is some controversy about this method, it is still a smart way to boost a company's Facebook post to increase your visibility and opportunity for interaction with your audience. When you recognize your target market, you will key in by enhancing your articles to those you wish to hit. Boosted articles are items that are compensated for being higher up on the news feed of a viewer. The cost will rely on how many users you want to access the message, and the reward will rely on how many views the article receives over time. You don't want to improve a single post you share on Facebook so you can raise stuff like competitions and extremely successful messages. You are going to want to look at improving articles because:

1. It will also market the goods or services that your company or corporation provides.

2. It'll promote visits to the website of the business.

3. It is going to spread awareness of a limited-time promotion that you manage.

* TO GAIN IDEAS FOR VIEWERS.

This tip goes for, and for a really good cause, crowdsourcing responses. The updates, messages, feedback, and other forms of interaction you find on the Facebook page of your company can provide you with important knowledge you need to remember. You will see what kind of content the audience can react to, what kind of content they can skip, and you will be able to decide what content you will concentrate on. You would now be able to pin down what the target is, and concentrate on the population. Through their User Feedback page, Facebook makes things extremely easy for you, where you can see what your community is engaged with. You'll know whether more text, pictures, or videos need to be shared and what sound these updates will have.

** GIVE THEM MATERIAL WHICH IS EXCLUSIVE AND MEANINGFUL.

This may seem a little simplistic, but the number of companies and products depending on the knowledge that is outdated or obsolete indicates how many missed opportunities Facebook has to deliver. Ideally, you've under-stood who your target customer and viewer is, so you need to consider care-fully the information they'll find most useful to you. Very definitely a young, suburban girl won't care about the Four Ways to Buy Tomatoes. Your common sense would support you with such issues, but taking an extra second to stop and think about your audience would help you out a lot and place you above the competition. Note, it's exclusive to your company or name. It doesn't matter that you do or don't have direct competition, there are items your product or service offers that no one else can say, so take advantage of them and show them through your Facebook page. Is there stuff that customers can't do due to your company before they can? Display pictures of them doing certain stuff, or provide videos to help someone with your product or service. If you're an expert in your field, use your Facebook page to give them tips and advice. The options are almost infinite, but take the time to sit down and talk about how special your company and goods from your rivals are, and then show them in your blogs.

* BUILDINGS OF YOUR VIEWER.

While the previous segment was about reaching the current audience and perhaps a couple of new members of the audience, what about developing the audience seriously in the beginning? Let's take a look at some ideas on how to get this done.

* ACTIONSPROUT ACCOUNT CREATION.

Many viewers agree why Facebook's main battlefield isn't the Facebook website, nor the news feeds. In reality, very few users actively visit the website; they connect with the website notifications in their news feeds, instead. The trouble with Facebook's most popular applications is they allow a customer to access the website. A photo contest would entail, for example, that the participant visits a special tab on the company's Facebook page to upload their photo and submit their contest entry. Therefore, to participate in the contest, they would abandon their news feed, which is their home away from home. ActionSprout can overcome this hurdle by encouraging you to bring in their news feeds the transaction operation. For example, in their news feeds a consumer can sign a petition, endorse projects, or ask for challenges. In their change, when they click on the operation, they are led to a single page where they complete the task. This is not meant to replace the custom tabs, but as a versatile complement to your custom tabs, it is better used.

* ANNOUNCEMENTS FOR NEW PRODUCTS IMPROVE.

Facebook boost posts are still very successful, particularly for smaller companies. While most experts would warn you not to use the app, small businesses will benefit greatly from boost posts announcing new items. Just because a lot of people who teach social media warn you not to raise messages, that doesn't imply they don't work or they don't work. Question all, and check yourself with the strategies and techniques.

* CUSTOM VIEWERS ON WEBSITE.

Facebook is evolving into what's regarded as a pay-to-play platform, and advertisers would continue to consider strategies to satisfy their audiences deeper. Although you can advertise targeting individual followers, one of Facebook's greatest advertisement strategies is to use personalized crowds on the Internet instead. You will run Facebook advertising via the Power Editor by utilizing Web site Custom Audiences. This helps you to track people who have viewed your website while they are back on Twitter, or a similar link on the internet. That's useful for several different purposes. Let's presume someone on the page is reading a book. If you're operating Website Custom Viewers, they'll see a sample to import from your guide when they go back to Facebook instead of having their usual page updates. When anyone posts an article on using one of your items, they will be contacted on Facebook with a connection to a video regarding how to use that product on their Facebook news page. Although these are only a handful of forms in which you can use this method to boost your Facebook marketing, there are several more out there. Being innovative about how you approach your market is the main lesson. Through the Facebook marketing campaigns, you will create more leads and more buyers, if you move above the usual.

** AUGMENT MARKETING EFFORTS.

With all that Facebook provides to its advertisers, it's possible to lose sight of the fact that it's a platform that promotes PR activities from your company. The reality is reporters depend on Facebook as a source of stories and Facebook endorses the site as a Rolodex of reporters getting a billion contacts. Where the company may have traditionally relied on a press release, you can now post the story on Facebook. It' is a low-friction alternative for covering the truth while breaking news or reflecting on current topics that can help you deliver the tale closer to the media and the public. Using Facebook Graph Search you will study media members. This method allows you to easily find out who is employed where, what blogs and publications your followers may read, or follow anyone with a public title relevant to journalism. You will identify possible sources while you are looking for a journalist and the name of the media source. Furthermore, constantly tracking the target media's Facebook accounts may be a successful way to promote the company or logo as a source of news. Most television outlets can use their social network pages to lobby sources. Within one place, you will create a note list of your chief pages to be constantly watching them.

** SPLIT FACEBOOK ADVERTISING TO CHECK.

Facebook ads have been crucial to corporations' marketing campaigns and doing it effectively without spending resources ensures you need to identify the right keywords. The way that you will achieve it is by dividing research audiences. Split research takes a proportion of the promotional budget and performs ads by modifying only one thing at a time and evaluating the outcomes to see which commercial was stronger. The Facebook ad promotions layout has improved a bit, so you will now turn on and off the advertising at the Ad Setpoint. Structure the ads to run one ad below each ad range so you can turn them on and off quickly at their specified times. Many people like to ask how big their target demographic is meant to be, but that would rely on other variables, and this query is not addressed correctly. Some individuals profit from reaching small markets, and other people gain from reaching limited populations, and some are safer targeting wider audiences. Split testing would be the only way for your brand to decide the reaction. Determine how well your ad can do by looking at the one that gets the cheapest clicks on whatever your ad's target is. If your ad attracts users to your page, you'll get the cheapest clicks on the platform. Create a conversion pixel to see which ad translates better on the website, if you are willing. Split research doesn't have to be costly or complicated because in the future it'll save you a lot of time. When you are willing to try five to ten potential markets for each commercial for twenty-five to fifty bucks, so you can have two or three ideal target groups for possible advertising.

PROMOTIONS AND CONTESTS:
MANAGING FACEBOOK.

◆◇◆

Facebook has been claiming for years that ads and competitions will be managed by apps and not on lists, or partitions, as people used to name them. Companies were not allowed to invite anyone to vote, or want a photo or a message to win. All that has changed, however.

Facebook also confirmed that they would now modify their terms to make it easy for companies to create and operate Facebook promotions. Pages are making competitions and ads run on their timelines. Organizations can now obtain entrants by making anyone tweet, click, or vote on a page or article, according to Facebook.

Through making the users contact the page they will gather entries, and they can use the likes as a voting method. Businesses with Facebook accounts today have several more choices, so by uploading a picture or text so inviting people to like or comment on that post they can run a contest easily. Through running the competitions, you will get even more attention on your website.

Contest and Promotion Rules.

1. When you use Facebook to manage or coordinate a campaign, you are liable for the legal execution of the campaign, including the of-

ficial laws, the eligibility criteria, and conditions of service, accordance with the legislation and guidelines regulating the promotion and prizes given.

2. Facebook promotions must include a full Facebook release from each user or entrant, and an acknowledgment that the campaign is not in any manner supported, funded, or operated from Facebook – or even associated with Facebook.

3. Promotions may be performed in Facebook applications, or on Facebook accounts. Individual timelines cannot be used to manage a contest - 'share your timeline for entry' or 'share the timeline of your buddy for entries.'

4. Facebook does not help with managing the campaign, so the organization acknowledges that it must do it at its own expense if it requires the software to execute the promo.

TWITTER FOR BUSINESS.

— ◆ ◇ ◆ —

W hen it comes to Twitter marketing, it is very important to have your bio and audience. We'll look at how you can maximize the performance with Twitter by taking a few simple steps.

* Make the Bio perfect. You want to ensure that all of the company's branding and personality are well known. This means having a bio which informs the viewer who you are, and which includes a link to the website of the organization or its landing page. Have a consistent tone between your Twitter account and the home page, and the viewer knows exactly who you are and what you are doing.

* Find out focus region influencers and specialists and communicate frequently with them. Using Twitter search or apps like Topsy to figure out where related opportunities, influencers, and consumers are by looking for keywords that contribute to your business. Then follow them, and daily interactions with them. You will list the top 100 most influential businesses and people in your field – authors, analysts, potential clients, writers and blogs, potential partners, etc. So add them to your private Twitter account, and connect daily with them. Apps like Hootsuite can make the task easier to manage. Remember to be constructive rather than advertising, and informal. Establish a relationship with these people, and explore opportunities for collaboration.

* Involve the coworkers. The first individuals who will help you build the brand should come from inside the company. Make sure staff connect on Facebook and interact with content by sharing, retweeting, and posting.

* Daily post. Daily tweeting is a sign of having a safe, engaging profile. If you just post once a week, or even once a month, you won't keep up with people on Facebook, or worse, people will forget you. Random messages and meetings are an ideal way to stay in front of clients. Only make sure that you tweet relevant information which is helpful to them. We share, add, or prefer your links, that way.

* Ask for Support on Facebook. Ask your followers to retweet, reference, or favorite tweets, or post fresh tweets with their posts. People like to think they are promoting their favorite brands, so don't be afraid to ask them to get the message out there for some support.

* Mentions and React to Log. You need to log keywords and company references and make sure you know what they're doing. Make sure you respond in a competent, polite manner if the response is acceptable at all. Customer service is the best marketing tool you have and many customers will be posting on Twitter their complaints and questions about products. You want to be there to show you can be of assistance. Set up your searches on Twitter for words that are important to your company. In these queries, track the conversations and step in when necessary. Of instance, if you're a dentist, you might set up a dentist search phrase in your city on Twitter, say Philadelphia, and the search word will be 'Dentist Philadelphia.' Then, when you see somebody tweeting they need to go to the dentist, but it's hard to get an appointment, you can step in to let them know you've got slots available for new patients.

* Update. You shouldn't be afraid to retweet, as this helps you connect and cement your thinking leadership in the industry in which you are. Oh, people love it when businesses retweet their posts!

* Tweets favorite. Many people don't know how tweet preferences work, but it gets more attention than a retweet or a comment from someone.

* After Hashtags or Patterns. You will look at trending hashtags and issues to find out how to relate to your brand in a relevant way. Through positioning your company in the trending topics, your handle will be seen while people are searching for tweets about that particular topic. Tagging articles with some themes and related hashtags can help you reach new users. Nonetheless, hashtags need to be used sparingly, because when they are overused or added to something that is not important, users see them as Twitter spam.

* Special Product Offers and Promotions. Hold any Twitter competitions, such as, the next fifty users who retweet this article will get a 50% off voucher or make them share their photos with the drug or in the store and have a random drawing.

* Use Images and Recordings. Using the videos and pictures to get visual. They receive three or four times more Twitter clicks than email messages. Images and videos have proved to earn more likes, impressions, and shares than a tweeter of plain text. While a community manager may do a good job engaging fans, a post about enjoying the weekend is far less successful than in-stream content where someone can see a film trailer and find out where the film is played in their neighborhood. In reality, analysis has shown that rich tweets have much fewer negative feedback ratings as consumers enjoy advertising on their mobile devices which is simpler to see.

* Foster posts. You want to participate in sponsored tweets because it addresses the followers specifically. Failure to describe who you are trying to reach will cost you a great deal of money and time. But be sure that your sponsored tweets aren't spammy. The aim is to provide value that creates your followers' reputation and confidence, not trick people into clicking on a link. Keep it cool. See to it that your promoted tweets don't run too long. If you want to keep delivering the word to your fans, then find a different, fresh way to say it.

* To integrate Twitter with other marketing efforts. As with other social media platforms, when it is combined with other marketing activities, Twitter is much more successful. For example, if you have a campaign or contest on Twitter, let your email subscribers know about it because they are another source of clients who have already let you know that they want to receive messages from you. When you regularly tweet a connection to your mailing list, you can use your email list to bind your Twitter account.

* Use the Analytics on Twitter. Just as you should use the built-in analytics from Facebook, you should use their native analytics to get an idea of what is and what isn't with your audience. You will see in the analytics dashboard what your strongest tweeting days are, the type of content you like, and the profiles of the followers your company draws. You can then repeat what does, and reassess what doesn't work.

TWITTER PLAN MARKETING.

Twitter is a bit different from other social media platforms so before you start building your following, we'll go over a fast strategy.

#1: SET TARGETS. You must determine what you want to do before you formulate your Twitter campaign. If you would like to see more people viewing company material, the target should include:

* Generate leads by having clicks on the landing page from the supporters.

* Build recognition of a new service or product by using Twitter to advertise it to possible interested clients or consumers;

* Use resources like Twitter's PR app, create a positive image of the company, services, and products.

* reate a group of like-minded people to give you feedback on how to develop a company, product, or marketing strategy.

* Improve customer support through the delivery of valuable content and one-on-one interactions that help customers make the most of services and products.

* Participate with business influencers in forums and develop credibility by an exchange of opinions.

#2: FIND OUT WHERE TWITTERS WORK INTO THE PLAN ON CONTENT. Your Twitter campaign, in your marketing strategy, will have its own unique identity. For starters, in your bigger plan, some of the items your Twitter strategy can do are: Traffic – you can use Twitter to drive traffic to a business website or blog, and use direct links to articles and landing pages.

* Transformations – you can use Twitter to combine tweets where you are looking for a particular action, such as sign-up or registration.

* Marketing – Twitter can be used to boost sales through photos, videos, and blog posts.

#3: IDENTIFY THE CORE FACEBOOK AUDIENCES. You need to learn what your target audience is before you create an audience. There are so many ways to come to grips with this. To keep track of specific demographics that like those types of content, you can create Twitter lists for every section of your audience.

* Search for keywords in your bios-use apps like Followerwonk or SocialBro to scan for people with keywords in their bios. You can also scan by venue.

* Look through hashtags – using trade-related hashtags and search feeds to assess who's watching them. Brainstorming sessions can help you find the best Marketing Strategy hashtags.

* Engage and track – use Twitter software to insert Twitter lists into tables, such as Tweetdeck and Hootsuite. This allows managing lists and building relationships with the others in the list faster.

#4: SET BEST TIMES FOR POST. Not everybody will be on Twitter 24 hours a day, seven days a week. When most of your fans are online, you have to find out, and that is when you will tweet. Many issues that you should remember are where you are based, and whether your followers are on daytime or night time. Here's how to figure out the best messaging hours for the most interaction:

* SocialBro – analyses the accounts of those who follow your business account and produces reports that show you when you should post to meet them.

* Auto schedule Hootsuite – if you're using Hootsuite, this app already recognizes the days the tweets get the most interaction.

* Tweriod – this analyses fans and tells them when they're off, as well as the optimal messaging times to hit them. #5 Having Ideas for the material. Twitter is the preferred destination for most content marketers to get great ideas on the subject. Try those tactics if you need to ponder on the next blog post or eBook subject.

* Include keywords – insert keywords that are important to your company and test what's listed. There might be a lot of different posts, forums, updates, and more that's going on right before you. These will show you what's common, what your target audience needs, and what influencers they chat with.

* Join the network – fans tweet about the business in which you are and can send you some great ideas. For instance, if you see people asking a lot of questions about a particular strategy, you could write tutorials about that.

* Search for the pain points – the potential customers and partners have concerns and issues. They may be seeking to get interested on Twitter and get a response. Keep an eye on what's going on to know what concerns you will be addressing.

#6: MONITOR TWEETS FOR THE COMPETITOR. Twitter is a very popular brand network and makes it easier to see what is going on in the market. Track their customers to see what gives them the most customer engagement.

* Join the opponents-technically, you don't have to pursue them. Make a private list which only you can see. Add the competitors, and if there is more than one primary account you can include competitor employees.

* Monitor commitments – know what people are saying about them, and how they are responding.

* Look at the posts that they publish – whether they produce a lot of material, this will let you see how they sell their content and how it is viewed by their community.

#7 CHOOSE WHAT YOU SAY. You should share a variety of content and not just text posts on Twitter. The network can support a lot of different media types that can be inserted into tweets, such as:

* Text – this nice, fast, and easy medium of tweeting is perfect for news, notifications, asking questions, and instant details.

* Images – that's a good way to improve the post. Images are going to stand out more, get more feedback on your posts, and more contributions.

* Videos – if the picture is worth a thousand words, then millions will be spoken. Videos embedded in messages work wonders to put messages before the appropriate audience. Embed your followers with a fast and insightful photo.

* SlideShare-this is a visual information aid but doesn't limit the displays on one screen. You can offer more material in a simple to consume ways with a slide deck.

* Links – if there is a valuable piece of business-related content on your website or elsewhere, insert a link or simply post it on your list. To raise visibility, attach a hashtag, and give a clear picture of what the connection would lead to.

#8: ADVERTISING MATERIAL. You can drive a lot of traffic to your website if you use Twitter well. But just tweeting the blog post title with a link back to the website will not work through time. When you create tweets to support blog images, articles, and material, you have to be imaginative. Here are some ways to get more clicks.

* Make it short – messages of a hundred characters or less often get better conversions. Write a brief introduction before promoting a link; it should be enough just to let the user know what to expect after clicking on the connection.

* Cite blogs - consider using the posts' teasers. The quotation should be factual and should give the reader a good idea of what the article is about.

* Use numbers – people love percentages and evidence, so use the data in your post to support your arguments. That gives substance to the concepts.

* Use the hashtags – this is an ideal way to reach those business leaders who have not yet adopted you. To do this, use the popular industry ones. You can use branded hashtags and encourage others to use them as well.

* Use the @mentions – make sure that you include them in the ads if your article references a website or a business influencer. They will be flattered and there's a good chance they'll share it too, so you'll reach a whole new audience.

* Call for updates – this is a great way to get retweeted messages. Only query the viewers to get the message retweet. Tweets which directly require retweets will probably get them.

* Encourage tweets-Promote your tweets for a small investment if you want more publicity than you already have. They're easy to make and will carry a lot of traffic to you.

* AUDIENCE-BUILDING. Whether it's from scratch or an existing following somewhere, creating and sustaining the following may appear time-consuming particularly to those familiar with the marketing. It's not enough to post many times a day to promote production. That is why it is important that you actively try to grow your daily Twitter audience. You have to grasp and be clear about your expectations to see the true progress with as little time as possible. If you establish and execute this schedule, you will continue to see more dramatic and rapid development in the market within as little as half an hour a day.

* TOTAL PLAN. The idea behind this active growth of the audience is to go out on Twitter and discover the users who are interested in your industry and niche, and target those who are in the midst of conversations about your topic and your industry. And you put yourself in a non-spam way in the center of this discussion that brings meaning to their discussion. For starters, if you have an online store page selling guitars, you might look for Twitter users discussing guitars or inquiring about how to play them, and then interact with them. Don't pitch them on, invite them to search the page, or invite them to adopt. Aid them, please. We can test you out more times than not and see who you are, see your profile, and click on the button to your website. They might even be watching you. There is a little bit more to it than that, like supporting and promoting the specific people, but in general, interacting with others who may be involved in your goods or services and contributing some relevance to their conversations. It may seem a little more underdog than you're used to, but it works.

* **EXPAND THAT BIO.** After you interact with someone first, they'll probably click on your profile to learn more about who you are. First impressions are everything, so make sure to optimize your Twitter bio and profile for that good first impression. The first aspect you ought to provide is an instantly recognizable profile image such that when you show in their update list when you have followed them, endorsed them, or reacted to a tweet, it's completely apparent who you are and what you're for.

For more memorable and relevant images, brands should forgo the logos. For instance, if you're a guitar store then use a guitar picture. The next thing you can remember is your username or your name on Twitter. If you are interested in getting a guitar player to look at your profile on Twitter when they see you in the notifications, you need a name identifiable to them.

For starters, if the name of your shop is Rad, then a better name on Twitter could be Rad Guitar rather than Rad, as guitar players will see Guitar in the name and want to know more about yourself. You will end up using threaded messages to help encourage people to join you. What do you want to let them know after they have clicked to view your profile once you have shown up in their notifications? Why is it that they should follow you rather than someone else? Who do you still talk about? Your pinned Tweet helps you to speak a bit more in-depth about yourself than your profile does. It can be used to submit users with profiles to landing pages where they can also receive emails.

YOUTUBE USING.

———————— ◆ ◇ ◆ ————————

Y ouTube provides somewhat close numbers to Facebook's. Every month they have one billion active users, which is around one of every two people on the internet. Users scan YouTube for educational and entertainment purposes. This ensures marketers can quickly get in front of their consumer with a quick YouTube channel or any videos demonstrating how to use their goods, or what their programs will do for their consumers. How are you using Twitch, then? Let's look at a few key points before you continue when it comes to posting videos to YouTube.

**Video-length. For example, YouTube lets you capture videos for up to 15 minutes. If you want to make a longer picture, you can go to the Upload page and click on the button 'increase your cap.' YouTube asks you to use a cellular phone to test your record. Verify that your software is up to date, so you can access the larger images. Nevertheless, a longer video is not necessarily better. If you're focusing on educational content, it may be difficult to fit it all in a couple of minutes; nevertheless, the videos you see most appear to be less than five minutes. So don't be afraid to start your experience with some small, snappy videos on YouTube instead of waiting until you have time to make longer ones.

* Model photo. When you make a video on YouTube, you must focus on the content that your customers, customers, and fans are looking to see. This ensures that your videos need to be tailored to their needs. When did you call your mate last week, to encourage them to watch the Home Shopping

Network? Videos that appear as though they were an infomercial are less likely to be posted. Providing knowledge and ideas that can be needed by others for their company or personal usage may improve the possibility of sharing the film. Place yourself in your position as a specialist and using YouTube as your tool for long-term public relations, instead of only focusing on a deal. Aside from giving strategies and suggestions, YouTube is a perfect spot to share any testimonials from customers. Written testimonials are difficult, so it's impossible to find out whether a particular individual made the testimonial. On the other side, videos render the testimonial to the person even more compelling. A far more compelling testimonial of the guy. YouTube videos can be used to provide office tours, show event looks behind the scenes, or give biographies of business leaders and employees. You can interview industry leaders you are in or record a presentation for people who can't attend a meeting. When you want clients and consumers to see images that you have made in the background without your image, so make screen shares so they will see and post those photos to YouTube afterward. You may also stream directly to a YouTube channel a Google+ hangout, or a virtual webinar.

* Apparatus. When you are on a small budget you can use a flip cam or a webcam to continue. Make sure you have clear, natural lighting for your ears, film in a dark environment, and use headphones to eliminate background noise.

* Sign Up. When you have one, you will sign up with a current Gmail account to register with YouTube. It seamlessly works with Google+ and helps you to access Google Hangouts. You will still sign up for every other email address you already have. While choosing your username and channel name, make sure that you choose your company name or a common term or

expression that refers to your industry. Your publicity documents will contain the URL for your website. Make sure to include a rundown of the channel and a teaser to make viewers appreciate what the channel is about, and what to anticipate. To customize your profile on YouTube, make sure you have your website link at the start of the video description and your profile's About Us portion. If you place that at the bottom of the page, fewer viewers will see it because they would need to press on the 'away' button to read the remainder of the video description. Furthermore, make sure that you are using the HTTP:/ in front of your URL, and it is a clickable connection. Otherwise, the viewers can go to the URL, rendering it a page that can be linked on. Otherwise, the viewers would have to break the connection into their browser and paste it in. Once you sign up you'll be able to pick a different label for your app.

* Pictures and Colors. In the channel settings, you can select your background color and picture under the appearances tab. A graphic designer is a good individual to employ to adjust your logo for the backdrop and other photos that are essential to your market. Select a color that matches the colors of your company. You should customize your layout in the featured link in addition to selecting the background image or colors. The segment on tabs would help you to decide whether the channel would show up for everyone, so make sure to check at the different choices and pick the one you'd choose.

* Edit. YouTube has some nice editing tools in the 'play stream' mode to enhance the images. Using the auto-fix feature, enhancements will allow you to improve your video quality, play with the lighting, change your video style, blur faces, and correct stabilizer shakiness. The annotations may be used to attach connections to sites, images, and playlists, or even encourage viewers to subscribe to the file. Alternatively, in the video editor area, you

can add any royalty-free music to your images, or splice clips from multiple videos.

* After a Video Upload. The video title is a video headline so it should be clear and concise. Make sure that the first two sentences of your summary contain keywords so that people who are looking for that specific information will find it. Google and Bing can check for appropriate terms on the first few phrases in the definition. Using tags to define the content of your video, both general and unique. Next, put the most appropriate ones, then ask yourself what keywords your viewers could use to locate a picture. Make sure you have connections to your playlists and platforms and let users know how to sign up.

**Running images. If you have a few videos on your page, you will pick one or even a couple of them for the videos to be included. When they have viewed those certain images, you may encourage the followers to watch more content. Just fill in the description with links or titles of those videos.

* Videos to share. If you have others your videos should be posted on all your social media platforms. That makes others see and share your stuff. Underneath your video, there is a sharing button that lets you share it on the news feed for social networking, or you can include a copy in your newsletter. Click the 'download script' button to add videos to your website, highlight the code given, and copy it to your site's HTML editor. You can adjust the video's size so that it suits best on your web. Don't fail to try to share the video with audiences. As the subscription list expands this occurs more naturally, but ask the main supporters to share your video to expand the list before you have a massive following.

* Resetting data. You want to make sure that the videos are available so that everyone will see them. And, whether you can know whether you want to

use it or not, or if it can require further editing, you can create private images. You may build unlisted videos if you choose to display a video only to those that have ties. You may pick which operation you want to share in the tabs section of the profile. You may select which operation you want to display in the profile tabs region. You can, for example, make statements regarding certain private or public videos.

* Shows. YouTube presents you with videos that you can access and find out how the material works. Clicking on the 'Analytics' section on your channel dashboard next to your Video Manager tab lets you display detailed details and viewers detail. It will let you see your channel's top ten viewed episodes, as well as positions for replay and demographics. You can see the statistics underneath the videos by clicking on the button 'statistics.' This will let you see the gender and age of the audience who's viewing your videos, as well as where they're located when they viewed. Use these metrics along with other measures, such as social network views, the amount of users who visit the page directly from posts, as well as direct reactions to email updates, allows you to create stronger ads over time which can be an integral part of a complex marketing campaign.

HOW TO CREATE A VIDEO

You can make engaging and fun videos to host your business on your YouTube channel with just a bit of an investment and some tools. Sharing videos via social networking, your profile, and through your emails helps get you new clients and consumers, and helps hold your loyal fans alive.

* Keep Fresh Content. YouTube's most prominent networks are the ones with a large amount of regularly updated material. If you intend to use the videos as a marketing device, you need a ton of images. There are lots of forms for a small company to create video material. Webinars and webcasts can be broken up and posted as series, and you can repurpose your infographics to videos that explain a topic, or you can make short tutorials or demonstrations of the product. Talk about having a background or profile video of a product. You will question colleagues, clients, or yourself.

* Call to Action included. You would most definitely have links in the explanation of the video, but before uploading the video, you will think about how you would like your viewers to react. Make sure the video contains the calls to practices. Possible calls for action may involve calling the organization for more details, subscribing to the website, posting the video on social networking platforms, providing suggestions, or some other requested action you may have.

* Recover Digital. When viewers watch the video they will rate the content and make feedback regarding it. To keep the momentum moving, track the input, and react as soon as possible. If you can tailor answers to the guests, such as answering questions or responding in any way to the message they left.

* Adjust Network. When you click on your tag, the YouTube page your visitors see is your site, so it shouldn't look like some other YouTube page out there. You may customize colors, ties, pictures, related facts, etc. It is an ideal way to strengthen messaging with color palettes, slogans, and mottos so that viewers can connect its advertisement with your market or business.

* Insert Thinking in Titles. People are hunting for YouTube the same way they are searching for Twitter – utilizing phrases and keywords to explain what they're hunting for. Titles are highly weighted on YouTube and in search engines but don't make it anything dull and non-descriptive. Instead, have the quality of the video in the headline, such as '10 ways to save time with (your company's) software.'

* *Choose the correct tags and groups. When posting videos to YouTube, you will pick a category and add tags that are also keywords for the film. You can pick from fifteen groups, and you'll add hundreds of tags to your photo. Beginning with the tags that YouTube recommends for you is fine since they are focused on what people normally look for. You may also manually apply some extra tags and variants on certain tags. When you are marketing dog goods, for example, you might include 'puppy' and 'dogs.'

* *Write Good Descriptions. YouTube's video explanations should be detailed yet brief, which should include several uses. Describe the video in a sentence or two, and provide a guide for those who want to learn more about your company website.

* Let's talk to clients. Small companies get amazing outcomes when they share customer testimonial videos on their YouTube page. It is a perfect opportunity to create trust and faith for anyone who might like a little 'nudge' to check out a good or service that you are selling. It is proven that

video testimonials have a far stronger effect on the viewers than a published version.

* Use Subheadings. It's pretty easy to allow subtitles on your YouTube video. Only switch on the auto-captioning and select the specific subtitles that pop up. There are millions of hearing disabled YouTube people who enjoy the captions you're introducing because they're free and they don't annoy the audiences who don't like them. On the other side, an audience can get offended by an annotation. Resist including such photo popups. Alternatively, place on the overview links to the feedback you have.

* Don't Confine YouTube Images. Only because you're building a YouTube channel, that doesn't imply many users should be hunting for it. Only make sure you share the news about the site as part of your campaign. You want to share new videos with us, write blog posts about them, or tweet the connect, or maybe upload it on Facebook. You can insert videos, especially product demos and tutorials, into your website.

TYPES OF VIDEOS TO MAKE.

Just in case you are always curious about what sorts of videos you should share for your business or niche, let's look at a couple of ideas to help out.

Photo review – YouTube lets you demonstrate your goods in practices. It is particularly helpful for businesses that have minimal traditional delivery outlets, like those that prefer to sell over the internet instead of in brick and mortar shops. Brands use YouTube to help consumers see why their goods are being utilized until they make the buying decision.

Activity and Marketing Highlights – YouTube helps you to remember positive activities by showcasing them to others who were unable to participate, or to others who would prefer to share with their mates where they were. If you run an event you can use your YouTube channel to share highlights. Just make sure everyone signed a release in the picture, or blur their faces.

Address Consumer Issues – Many businesses want to use YouTube to address consumer issues for their products. They could, for example, post a video of how to install a device, or a screenshot demo demonstrating how to use similar apps. Videos are a perfect way to work with often asked issues, troubleshoot challenges, or simply create the brand. YouTube is a perfect place to show your consumers that you are an authority in your field and help people understand your market.

CONCLUSION

———————◆◇◆———————

With its groundbreaking content discovery algorithm, TikTok has helped to create an immense video-first network that connects people from all ages around the globe. User-generated content-apps are just as good as the platform content. It would, therefore, be unfair not to praise TikTok's video editing toolkit, which enables its creators to make this engaging content. If filters were the secret to getting better Instagram images. Then it would be fair to say that the key to unlocking more engaging TikTok videos has been music and captions. I should advise content producers to prepare for a strong rewatch and completion if I were to offer advice to those trying to create quality content on TikTok. The latest clickbait is excitement, comprehension, and expectation. We'd like to get input on this article, and would love to include your suggestions so please email us.

* Keep in mind The target market. The very first law of social networking etiquette emphasizes the value of being an engaging participant in a conversation. Social networking networks can provide useful knowledge so individuals will exchange with others, and from several outlets, it can be accessed. You want to be aware of what kind of content is most appealing to your audience, and what kind of content should not be posted. Keep in mind what kind of social media account you would like to follow if not yours. Deliver the content you're talking about in your description of the profile, and do it at the right time to avoid spamming followers

* Respond to Comments. Communication on a social network is designed to be a two-way street where you get real-time responses to messages, and when used in this way, social media is the most effective. Name someone to look through social media platforms and monitor for interactions, and make sure they interact back with those interactions. When you have a large amount of feedback regularly, it lets you set up an assessment framework and see which ones can be addressed instantly, and which ones should wait for a little. It should be able to go without saying however that all comments should be answered, particularly if they are negative. Ignoring a poor comment will result in a consumer failure or a very bad tragedy in public relations. Addressing critical reviews in a timely way will help transform critics into champions for the company.

Printed in Great Britain
by Amazon